Philosophy of Law: A Very Short Introduction

VERY SHORT INTRODUCTIONS are for anyone wanting a stimulating and accessible way in to a new subject. They are written by experts, and have been translated into more than 40 different languages.

The Series began in 1995, and now covers a wide variety of topics in every discipline. The VSI library now contains over 350 volumes—a Very Short Introduction to everything from Psychology and Philosophy of Science to American History and Relativity—and continues to grow in every subject area.

Very Short Introductions available now:

ADVERTISING Winston Fletcher
AFRICAN HISTORY John Parker and Richard Rathbone
AFRICAN RELIGIONS Jacob K. Olupona
AGNOSTICISM Robin Le Poidevin
AMERICAN HISTORY Paul S. Boyer
AMERICAN IMMIGRATION David A. Gerber
AMERICAN LEGAL HISTORY G. Edward White
AMERICAN POLITICAL PARTIES AND ELECTIONS L. Sandy Maisel
AMERICAN POLITICS Richard M. Valelly
THE AMERICAN PRESIDENCY Charles O. Jones
ANAESTHESIA Aidan O'Donnell
ANARCHISM Colin Ward
ANCIENT EGYPT Ian Shaw
ANCIENT GREECE Paul Cartledge
THE ANCIENT NEAR EAST Amanda H. Podany
ANCIENT PHILOSOPHY Julia Annas
ANCIENT WARFARE Harry Sidebottom
ANGELS David Albert Jones
ANGLICANISM Mark Chapman
THE ANGLO-SAXON AGE John Blair
THE ANIMAL KINGDOM Peter Holland
ANIMAL RIGHTS David DeGrazia
THE ANTARCTIC Klaus Dodds
ANTISEMITISM Steven Beller
ANXIETY Daniel Freeman and Jason Freeman
THE APOCRYPHAL GOSPELS Paul Foster
ARCHAEOLOGY Paul Bahn
ARCHITECTURE Andrew Ballantyne
ARISTOCRACY William Doyle
ARISTOTLE Jonathan Barnes
ART HISTORY Dana Arnold
ART THEORY Cynthia Freeland
ASTROBIOLOGY David C. Catling
ATHEISM Julian Baggini
AUGUSTINE Henry Chadwick
AUSTRALIA Kenneth Morgan
AUTISM Uta Frith
THE AVANT GARDE David Cottington
THE AZTECS Davíd Carrasco
BACTERIA Sebastian G. B. Amyes
BARTHES Jonathan Culler
THE BEATS David Sterritt
BEAUTY Roger Scruton
BESTSELLERS John Sutherland
THE BIBLE John Riches
BIBLICAL ARCHAEOLOGY Eric H. Cline
BIOGRAPHY Hermione Lee
THE BLUES Elijah Wald
THE BOOK OF MORMON Terryl Givens
BORDERS Alexander C. Diener and Joshua Hagen
THE BRAIN Michael O'Shea
THE BRITISH CONSTITUTION Martin Loughlin
THE BRITISH EMPIRE Ashley Jackson
BRITISH POLITICS Anthony Wright
BUDDHA Michael Carrithers
BUDDHISM Damien Keown
BUDDHIST ETHICS Damien Keown
CANCER Nicholas James
CAPITALISM James Fulcher
CATHOLICISM Gerald O'Collins

CAUSATION Stephen Mumford and Rani Lill Anjum
THE CELL Terence Allen and Graham Cowling
THE CELTS Barry Cunliffe
CHAOS Leonard Smith
CHILDREN'S LITERATURE Kimberley Reynolds
CHINESE LITERATURE Sabina Knight
CHOICE THEORY Michael Allingham
CHRISTIAN ART Beth Williamson
CHRISTIAN ETHICS D. Stephen Long
CHRISTIANITY Linda Woodhead
CITIZENSHIP Richard Bellamy
CIVIL ENGINEERING David Muir Wood
CLASSICAL MYTHOLOGY Helen Morales
CLASSICS Mary Beard and John Henderson
CLAUSEWITZ Michael Howard
CLIMATE Mark Maslin
THE COLD WAR Robert McMahon
COLONIAL AMERICA Alan Taylor
COLONIAL LATIN AMERICAN LITERATURE Rolena Adorno
COMEDY Matthew Bevis
COMMUNISM Leslie Holmes
THE COMPUTER Darrel Ince
THE CONQUISTADORS Matthew Restall and Felipe Fernández-Armesto
CONSCIENCE Paul Strohm
CONSCIOUSNESS Susan Blackmore
CONTEMPORARY ART Julian Stallabrass
CONTEMPORARY FICTION Robert Eaglestone
CONTINENTAL PHILOSOPHY Simon Critchley
COSMOLOGY Peter Coles
CRITICAL THEORY Stephen Eric Bronner
THE CRUSADES Christopher Tyerman
CRYPTOGRAPHY Fred Piper and Sean Murphy
THE CULTURAL REVOLUTION Richard Curt Kraus
DADA AND SURREALISM David Hopkins
DARWIN Jonathan Howard
THE DEAD SEA SCROLLS Timothy Lim
DEMOCRACY Bernard Crick
DERRIDA Simon Glendinning
DESCARTES Tom Sorell
DESERTS Nick Middleton
DESIGN John Heskett
DEVELOPMENTAL BIOLOGY Lewis Wolpert
THE DEVIL Darren Oldridge
DIASPORA Kevin Kenny
DICTIONARIES Lynda Mugglestone
DINOSAURS David Norman
DIPLOMACY Joseph M. Siracusa
DOCUMENTARY FILM Patricia Aufderheide
DREAMING J. Allan Hobson
DRUGS Leslie Iversen
DRUIDS Barry Cunliffe
EARLY MUSIC Thomas Forrest Kelly
THE EARTH Martin Redfern
ECONOMICS Partha Dasgupta
EDUCATION Gary Thomas
EGYPTIAN MYTH Geraldine Pinch
EIGHTEENTH-CENTURY BRITAIN Paul Langford
THE ELEMENTS Philip Ball
EMOTION Dylan Evans
EMPIRE Stephen Howe
ENGELS Terrell Carver
ENGINEERING David Blockley
ENGLISH LITERATURE Jonathan Bate
ENTREPRENEURSHIP Paul Westhead and Mike Wright
ENVIRONMENTAL ECONOMICS Stephen Smith
EPIDEMIOLOGY Rodolfo Saracci
ETHICS Simon Blackburn
ETHNOMUSICOLOGY Timothy Rice
THE EUROPEAN UNION John Pinder and Simon Usherwood
EVOLUTION Brian and Deborah Charlesworth
EXISTENTIALISM Thomas Flynn
FASCISM Kevin Passmore
FASHION Rebecca Arnold
FEMINISM Margaret Walters
FILM Michael Wood
FILM MUSIC Kathryn Kalinak
THE FIRST WORLD WAR Michael Howard
FOLK MUSIC Mark Slobin
FOOD John Krebs
FORENSIC PSYCHOLOGY David Canter
FORENSIC SCIENCE Jim Fraser
FOSSILS Keith Thomson
FOUCAULT Gary Gutting

FRACTALS Kenneth Falconer
FREE SPEECH Nigel Warburton
FREE WILL Thomas Pink
FRENCH LITERATURE John D. Lyons
THE FRENCH REVOLUTION William Doyle
FREUD Anthony Storr
FUNDAMENTALISM Malise Ruthven
GALAXIES John Gribbin
GALILEO Stillman Drake
GAME THEORY Ken Binmore
GANDHI Bhikhu Parekh
GENIUS Andrew Robinson
GEOGRAPHY John Matthews and David Herbert
GEOPOLITICS Klaus Dodds
GERMAN LITERATURE Nicholas Boyle
GERMAN PHILOSOPHY Andrew Bowie
GLOBAL CATASTROPHES Bill McGuire
GLOBAL ECONOMIC HISTORY Robert C. Allen
GLOBAL WARMING Mark Maslin
GLOBALIZATION Manfred Steger
THE GOTHIC Nick Groom
GOVERNANCE Mark Bevir
THE GREAT DEPRESSION AND THE NEW DEAL Eric Rauchway
HABERMAS James Gordon Finlayson
HAPPINESS Daniel M. Haybron
HEGEL Peter Singer
HEIDEGGER Michael Inwood
HERODOTUS Jennifer T. Roberts
HIEROGLYPHS Penelope Wilson
HINDUISM Kim Knott
HISTORY John H. Arnold
THE HISTORY OF ASTRONOMY Michael Hoskin
THE HISTORY OF LIFE Michael Benton
THE HISTORY OF MATHEMATICS Jacqueline Stedall
THE HISTORY OF MEDICINE William Bynum
THE HISTORY OF TIME Leofranc Holford-Strevens
HIV/AIDS Alan Whiteside
HOBBES Richard Tuck
HUMAN EVOLUTION Bernard Wood
HUMAN RIGHTS Andrew Clapham
HUMANISM Stephen Law
HUME A. J. Ayer
HUMOUR Noël Carroll
IDEOLOGY Michael Freeden
INDIAN PHILOSOPHY Sue Hamilton
INFORMATION Luciano Floridi
INNOVATION Mark Dodgson and David Gann
INTELLIGENCE Ian J. Deary
INTERNATIONAL MIGRATION Khalid Koser
INTERNATIONAL RELATIONS Paul Wilkinson
INTERNATIONAL SECURITY Christopher S. Browning
ISLAM Malise Ruthven
ISLAMIC HISTORY Adam Silverstein
ITALIAN LITERATURE Peter Hainsworth and David Robey
JESUS Richard Bauckham
JOURNALISM Ian Hargreaves
JUDAISM Norman Solomon
JUNG Anthony Stevens
KABBALAH Joseph Dan
KAFKA Ritchie Robertson
KANT Roger Scruton
KEYNES Robert Skidelsky
KIERKEGAARD Patrick Gardiner
THE KORAN Michael Cook
LANDSCAPES AND GEOMORPHOLOGY Andrew Goudie and Heather Viles
LANGUAGES Stephen R. Anderson
LATE ANTIQUITY Gillian Clark
LAW Raymond Wacks
THE LAWS OF THERMODYNAMICS Peter Atkins
LEADERSHIP Keith Grint
LINCOLN Allen C. Guelzo
LINGUISTICS Peter Matthews
LITERARY THEORY Jonathan Culler
LOCKE John Dunn
LOGIC Graham Priest
MACHIAVELLI Quentin Skinner
MADNESS Andrew Scull
MAGIC Owen Davies
MAGNA CARTA Nicholas Vincent
MAGNETISM Stephen Blundell
MALTHUS Donald Winch
MANAGEMENT John Hendry
MAO Delia Davin
MARINE BIOLOGY Philip V. Mladenov

THE MARQUIS DE SADE John Phillips
MARTIN LUTHER Scott H. Hendrix
MARTYRDOM Jolyon Mitchell
MARX Peter Singer
MATHEMATICS Timothy Gowers
THE MEANING OF LIFE Terry Eagleton
MEDICAL ETHICS Tony Hope
MEDICAL LAW Charles Foster
MEDIEVAL BRITAIN John Gillingham and Ralph A. Griffiths
MEMORY Jonathan K. Foster
METAPHYSICS Stephen Mumford
MICHAEL FARADAY Frank A. J. L. James
MODERN ART David Cottington
MODERN CHINA Rana Mitter
MODERN FRANCE Vanessa R. Schwartz
MODERN IRELAND Senia Pašeta
MODERN JAPAN Christopher Goto-Jones
MODERN LATIN AMERICAN LITERATURE Roberto González Echevarría
MODERN WAR Richard English
MODERNISM Christopher Butler
MOLECULES Philip Ball
THE MONGOLS Morris Rossabi
MORMONISM Richard Lyman Bushman
MUHAMMAD Jonathan A. C. Brown
MULTICULTURALISM Ali Rattansi
MUSIC Nicholas Cook
MYTH Robert A. Segal
THE NAPOLEONIC WARS Mike Rapport
NATIONALISM Steven Grosby
NELSON MANDELA Elleke Boehmer
NEOLIBERALISM Manfred Steger and Ravi Roy
NETWORKS Guido Caldarelli and Michele Catanzaro
THE NEW TESTAMENT Luke Timothy Johnson
THE NEW TESTAMENT AS LITERATURE Kyle Keefer
NEWTON Robert Iliffe
NIETZSCHE Michael Tanner
NINETEENTH-CENTURY BRITAIN Christopher Harvie and H. C. G. Matthew
THE NORMAN CONQUEST George Garnett
NORTH AMERICAN INDIANS Theda Perdue and Michael D. Green
NORTHERN IRELAND Marc Mulholland
NOTHING Frank Close
NUCLEAR POWER Maxwell Irvine
NUCLEAR WEAPONS Joseph M. Siracusa
NUMBERS Peter M. Higgins
OBJECTIVITY Stephen Gaukroger
THE OLD TESTAMENT Michael D. Coogan
THE ORCHESTRA D. Kern Holoman
ORGANIZATIONS Mary Jo Hatch
PAGANISM Owen Davies
THE PALESTINIAN-ISRAELI CONFLICT Martin Bunton
PARTICLE PHYSICS Frank Close
PAUL E. P. Sanders
PENTECOSTALISM William K. Kay
THE PERIODIC TABLE Eric R. Scerri
PHILOSOPHY Edward Craig
PHILOSOPHY OF LAW Raymond Wacks
PHILOSOPHY OF SCIENCE Samir Okasha
PHOTOGRAPHY Steve Edwards
PLAGUE Paul Slack
PLANETS David A. Rothery
PLANTS Timothy Walker
PLATO Julia Annas
POLITICAL PHILOSOPHY David Miller
POLITICS Kenneth Minogue
POSTCOLONIALISM Robert Young
POSTMODERNISM Christopher Butler
POSTSTRUCTURALISM Catherine Belsey
PREHISTORY Chris Gosden
PRESOCRATIC PHILOSOPHY Catherine Osborne
PRIVACY Raymond Wacks
PROBABILITY John Haigh
PROGRESSIVISM Walter Nugent
PROTESTANTISM Mark A. Noll
PSYCHIATRY Tom Burns
PSYCHOLOGY Gillian Butler and Freda McManus
PURITANISM Francis J. Bremer
THE QUAKERS Pink Dandelion
QUANTUM THEORY ohn Polkinghorne
RACISM Ali Rattansi
RADIOACTIVITY Claudio Tuniz
RASTAFARI Ennis B. Edmonds

THE REAGAN REVOLUTION Gil Troy
REALITY Jan Westerhoff
THE REFORMATION Peter Marshall
RELATIVITY Russell Stannard
RELIGION IN AMERICA Timothy Beal
THE RENAISSANCE Jerry Brotton
RENAISSANCE ART Geraldine A. Johnson
RHETORIC Richard Toye
RISK Baruch Fischhoff and John Kadvany
RIVERS Nick Middleton
ROBOTICS Alan Winfield
ROMAN BRITAIN Peter Salway
THE ROMAN EMPIRE Christopher Kelly
THE ROMAN REPUBLIC David M. Gwynn
ROMANTICISM Michael Ferber
ROUSSEAU Robert Wokler
RUSSELL A. C. Grayling
RUSSIAN HISTORY Geoffrey Hosking
RUSSIAN LITERATURE Catriona Kelly
THE RUSSIAN REVOLUTION S. A. Smith
SCHIZOPHRENIA Chris Frith and Eve Johnstone
SCHOPENHAUER Christopher Janaway
SCIENCE AND RELIGION Thomas Dixon
SCIENCE FICTION David Seed
THE SCIENTIFIC REVOLUTION Lawrence M. Principe
SCOTLAND Rab Houston
SEXUALITY Véronique Mottier
SHAKESPEARE Germaine Greer
SIKHISM Eleanor Nesbitt
THE SILK ROAD James A. Millward
SLEEP Steven W. Lockley and Russell G. Foster
SOCIAL AND CULTURAL ANTHROPOLOGY John Monaghan and Peter Just
SOCIALISM Michael Newman
SOCIOLINGUISTICS John Edwards
SOCIOLOGY Steve Bruce
SOCRATES C. C. W. Taylor
THE SOVIET UNION Stephen Lovell
THE SPANISH CIVIL WAR Helen Graham
SPANISH LITERATURE Jo Labanyi
SPINOZA Roger Scruton
SPIRITUALITY Philip Sheldrake
STARS Andrew King
STATISTICS David J. Hand
STEM CELLS Jonathan Slack
STUART BRITAIN John Morrill
SUPERCONDUCTIVITY Stephen Blundell
SYMMETRY Ian Stewart
TERRORISM Charles Townshend
THEOLOGY David F. Ford
THOMAS AQUINAS Fergus Kerr
THOUGHT Tim Bayne
TIBETAN BUDDHISM Matthew T. Kapstein
TOCQUEVILLE Harvey C. Mansfield
TRAGEDY Adrian Poole
THE TROJAN WAR Eric H. Cline
TRUST Katherine Hawley
THE TUDORS John Guy
TWENTIETH-CENTURY BRITAIN Kenneth O. Morgan
THE UNITED NATIONS Jussi M. Hanhimäki
THE U.S. CONGRESS Donald A. Ritchie
THE U.S. SUPREME COURT Linda Greenhouse
UTOPIANISM Lyman Tower Sargent
THE VIKINGS Julian Richards
VIRUSES Dorothy H. Crawford
WITCHCRAFT Malcolm Gaskill
WITTGENSTEIN A. C. Grayling
WORK Stephen Fineman
WORLD MUSIC Philip Bohlman
THE WORLD TRADE ORGANIZATION Amrita Narlikar
WRITING AND SCRIPT Andrew Robinson

Available soon:

BLACK HOLES Katherine Blundell
REVOLUTIONS Jack A. Goldstone
FAMILY LAW Jonathan Herring
THE ICE AGE Jamie Woodward
TEETH Peter S. Ungar

For more information visit our website
www.oup.com/vsi/

Raymond Wacks

PHILOSOPHY OF LAW

A Very Short Introduction

OXFORD
UNIVERSITY PRESS

OXFORD
UNIVERSITY PRESS

Great Clarendon Street, Oxford, OX2 6DP,
United Kingdom

Oxford University Press is a department of the University of Oxford.
It furthers the University's objective of excellence in research, scholarship,
and education by publishing worldwide. Oxford is a registered trade mark of
Oxford University Press in the UK and in certain other countries

First published 2006
Second Edition published 2014

Published in the United States of America by Oxford University Press
198 Madison Avenue, New York, NY 10016, United States of America

British Library Cataloguing in Publication Data
Data available

Library of Congress Control Number: 2013953524

ISBN 978–0–19–968700–8

Printed and bound by
CPI Group (UK) Ltd, Croydon, CR0 4YY

Preface

Brevity is not a virtue normally associated with the law, let alone its practitioners. Nor does its literature avoid the bulky and the long. Law books are weighty; and tomes on legal philosophy also incline to the stout and substantial. Perhaps this is an inescapable vice.

This series, however, obliges its authors to slim down, to compress, to abridge—without oversimplifying the subject of the book. Distilling the essentials of the philosophy of law is, needless to say, an ambitious, though I hope not an entirely quixotic, task. The purpose of this slender volume is to provide the general reader with a lively and accessible guide to the central questions of legal philosophy in its quest to illuminate the frequently elusive concept of law, and its relation to the universal questions of justice, rights, and morality.

The law is rarely out of the news. It frequently excites controversy. While lawyers and politicians celebrate the virtues of the rule of law, reformers lament its shortcomings, and cynics question its professed equivalence with justice. Yet all recognize the law as a vehicle for social change. And few doubt its central role in our social, political, moral, and economic life.

But what is this thing called law? Does it consist of a set of universal moral principles in accordance with nature (see

Chapter 1)? Or is it simply a collection of largely man-made, valid rules, commands, or norms (Chapter 2)? Does the law have a specific purpose, such as the protection of individual rights (Chapter 3), the attainment of justice (Chapter 4), or economic, political, and sexual equality (Chapter 6)? Can the law be divorced from its social context (Chapter 5)?

These are merely some of the questions that lie in wait for anyone attempting to uncover the meaning of the concept of law and its function and purpose. And they permeate the landscape of the philosophy of law with its generous frontiers. Charting this vast territory is a daunting assignment. I can hope, in these pages, to identify only the most prominent features of its topography. To this end, I have placed the emphasis upon the leading legal theories, for they provide the optimal introduction to both classical and contemporary jurisprudential thought.

Legal theory is a far cry from legal theatre. Yet even the most sensationalist criminal trials—real or manufactured—that have become regular television fare, encapsulate features of the law that characteristically agitate legal philosophers. They spawn awkward questions about moral and legal responsibility, the justifications of punishment, the concept of harm, the judicial function, due process, and many more. The philosophy of law, it is easy to demonstrate, is rarely an abstract, impractical pursuit.

We live in a troubled, inequitable world. Perhaps it has always been so. In the face of wickedness and injustice, it is not difficult to descend into vague oversimplification and rhetoric when reflecting upon the proper nature and function of the law. Analytical clarity and scrupulous jurisprudential deliberation on the fundamental nature of law, justice, and the meaning of legal concepts are indispensable. Legal theory has a decisive role to play in defining and defending the values and ideals that sustain our way of life.

The staff of Oxford University Press have, as always, been a pleasure to work with. I am particularly grateful to Emma Ma.

For her love, encouragement, and support, I owe a heavy debt of gratitude to my wife, Penelope, whose word is law.

Contents

List of illustrations

The publisher and authors apologize for any errors or omissions in the above list. If contacted they will be happy to rectify these at the earliest opportunity.

Chapter 1
Natural law

'It's just not right.' 'It's not natural.' How many times have you heard these sorts of judgements invoked against a particular practice or act? What do they mean? When abortion is pronounced immoral, or same-sex marriages unacceptable, what is the basis of this censure? (Figure 1). Is there an objectively ascertainable measure of right and wrong, good and bad? If so, by what means can we retrieve it?

Moral questions pervade our lives; they are the stuff of political, and hence legal, debate. Moreover, since the establishment of the United Nations, the ethical tenor of international relations, especially in the field of human rights, is embodied in an increasing variety of international declarations and conventions. Many of these draw on the unspoken assumption of natural law that there is indeed a corpus of moral truths that, if we apply our reasoning minds, we can all discover.

Ethical problems have, of course, preoccupied moral philosophers since Aristotle. The revival of natural law theory may suggest that we have, over the centuries, come no closer to resolving them.

'The best description of natural law', according to one leading natural lawyer, 'is that it provides a name for the point of

1. Homosexuality, same-sex marriages, and marital infidelity offend the principles of natural law

intersection between law and morals.' In his widely acclaimed book, *Natural Law and Natural Rights*, John Finnis asserts that when we attempt to explain what law is, we make assumptions, willy-nilly, about what is 'good':

> It is often supposed that an evaluation of law as a type of social institution, if it is to be undertaken at all, must be preceded by a value-free description and analysis of that institution as it exists in fact. But the development of modern jurisprudence suggests, and reflection on the methodology of any social science confirms, that a theorist cannot give a theoretical description and analysis of social facts, unless he also participates in the work of evaluation, of understanding what is really good for human persons, and what is really required by practical reasonableness.

This is a trenchant foundation for an analysis of natural law. It proposes that when we are discerning what is *good*, we are using our intelligence differently from when we are determining what *exists*. In other words, if we are to understand the nature and impact of the natural law project, we must recognize that it yields a different logic.

The Roman lawyer Cicero, drawing on Stoic philosophy, usefully identified the three main components of any natural law philosophy:

> True law is right reason in agreement with Nature; it is of universal application, unchanging and everlasting.... It is a sin to try to alter this law, nor is it allowable to attempt to repeal any part of it, and it is impossible to abolish it entirely.... [God] is the author of this law, its promulgator, and its enforcing judge.

This underlines natural law's universality and immutability, its standing as a 'higher' law, and its discoverability by reason (it is in this sense 'natural'). Classical natural law doctrine has been employed to justify both revolution and reaction. During the 6th century BC, the Greeks described human laws as owing their importance to the power of fate that controlled everything. This conservative view is easily deployed to justify even iniquitous aspects of the status quo. By the 5th century BC, however, it was acknowledged that there might be a conflict between the law of nature and the law of man.

Aristotle devoted less attention to natural law than to the distinction between natural and conventional justice. But it was the Greek Stoics, as mentioned above, who were particularly attracted to the notion of natural law, where 'natural' meant in accordance with reason. The Stoic view informed the approach adopted by the Romans (as expressed by Cicero) who recognized, at least in theory, that laws which did not conform to 'reason' might be regarded as invalid.

The Catholic Church gave expression to the full-blown philosophy of natural law, as we understand it today. As early as the 5th century, St Augustine asked, 'What are States without justice, but robber bands enlarged?' But the leading exposition of natural law is to be found in the writings of the Dominican St Thomas Aquinas (1225–74), whose principal work *Summa Theologiae* contains the most comprehensive statement of Christian doctrine on the subject. He distinguishes between four categories of law: the eternal law (divine reason known only to God), natural law (the participation of the eternal law in rational creatures, discoverable by reason), divine law (revealed in the scriptures), and human law (supported by reason, and enacted for the common good).

The 13th century saw the development of European city-states. The Pope's authority over these states was hampered through want of a theological standpoint in respect of the exercise of secular power. St Augustine had merely endorsed the Biblical exhortation to 'render... unto Caesar the things which are Caesar's'. But Aquinas deployed Aristotle's philosophy in an effort to reconcile secular and Christian authority. He argued that Christianity was a stage in the development of humanity that was unavailable to the Greeks. The *polis* in which we were destined to live was therefore Christian.

He argued that natural law is merely one element of divine providence: it is a 'participation' in the eternal law—the rational plan that orders all creation. In other words, it is the means by which rational beings participate in the eternal law. When human beings 'receive' natural law, its content comprises the principles of practical rationality by which human action is to be judged as reasonable or unreasonable. For Aquinas it is this characteristic of natural law that justifies its description as 'law', for law, he asserts, consists in rules of action declared by one who protects the interests of the community: since God defends and protects the universe, His decision to create rational beings with the capacity to act freely in accordance with reason entitles our regarding these principles as constituting 'law'.

The tenets of natural law are binding on us, Aquinas contends, because—as rational beings—we are guided towards them by nature; they point us toward the good, as well as towards certain specific goods. Furthermore, these principles are known to us by virtue of our nature: we exhibit this knowledge in our inherent aspiration to achieve the various goods that natural law exhorts us to pursue. We are able to discern the essence of practical knowledge, though the precise practical consequences of that understanding may often be difficult to determine. And, Aquinas acknowledges, our passion or malevolence may obstruct their application.

At the heart of Aquinas's elucidation of natural law is the elementary idea that good be done and evil avoided. Given his theological context of objective moral truth, Aquinas contends that we have a continuing duty to seek the good. We know intuitively what constitutes the good: it includes life, knowledge, procreation, society, and reasonable conduct. For him the good is prior to the right. Whether an act is right is less important than whether it achieves or is some good. We are, he suggests, capable of reasoning from these principles about goods to practical means by which to realize these goods.

How do we recognize when an act is fundamentally unsound? There is no simple yardstick; we must dissect features of the acts in question, such as their objects, their ends, their circumstances under which they are carried out. For example, Aquinas contends that certain acts may be defective by virtue of their intention: acting against a good occurs, for example, when one commits a murder, tells a lie, or blasphemes. Although he does not pronounce universal, absolute, eternal principles of right conduct, he does claim that natural law regards it as always wrong to kill the innocent, to lie, to blaspheme, or to indulge in adultery and sodomy, and that they are wrong is a matter of natural law.

One aspect of Aquinas's theory has attracted particular attention and controversy. He states that a 'law' that fails to conform to natural or divine law is not a law at all. This is usually expressed as *lex iniusta non est lex* (an unjust law is not law). However, modern scholars maintain that Aquinas himself never made this assertion, but merely quoted St Augustine. Plato, Aristotle, and Cicero also uttered comparable sentiments, yet it is a proposition that is most closely associated with Aquinas who seems to have meant that laws which conflict with the requirements of natural law lose their power to bind morally.

A government, in other words, that abuses its authority by enacting laws which are unjust (unreasonable or against the common good) forfeits its right to be obeyed because it lacks moral authority. Such a law Aquinas calls a 'corruption of law'. But he does not appear to support the view that one is always justified in disobeying an unjust law, for though he does declare that if a ruler enacts unjust laws 'their subjects are not obliged to obey them', he adds guardedly, 'except, perhaps, in certain special cases when it is a matter of avoiding scandal' (i.e. a corrupting example to others) or civil disorder. This is a far cry from the radical claims sometimes made in the name of Aquinas, which seek to justify disobedience to law.

By the 17th century in Europe, the exposition of entire branches of the law, notably public international law, purported to be founded on natural law. Hugo de Groot (1583–1645), or Grotius as he is generally called, is normally associated with the secularization of natural law. In his influential work, *De Jure Belli ac Pacis*, he asserts that, even if God did not exist, natural law would have the same content. This proved to be an important basis for the developing discipline of public international law. Presumably Grotius meant that certain things were 'intrinsically' wrong—whether or not God decrees them; for, to use Grotius's own analogy, even God cannot cause two times two not to equal four!

Natural law received a stamp of approval in England in the 18th century in Sir William Blackstone's *Commentaries on the Laws of*

England. Blackstone (1723–80) begins his great work by declaring that English law derives its authority from natural law. But, although he invokes this divine source of positive law, and even regards it as capable of nullifying enacted laws in conflict with natural law, his account of the law is not actually informed by natural law theory. Nevertheless, Blackstone's attempt to clothe the positive law with a legitimacy derived from natural law drew the fire of Jeremy Bentham who described natural law as, amongst other things, 'a mere work of the fancy' (see Chapter 2).

Aquinas is associated with a fairly conservative view of natural law. But the principles of natural law have been used to justify revolutions—especially the American and the French—on the ground that the law infringed individuals' natural rights. Thus in America the revolution against British colonial rule was based on an appeal to the natural rights of all Americans, in the lofty words of the Declaration of Independence of 1776, to 'life, liberty and the pursuit of happiness'. As the Declaration puts it, 'We hold these truths to be self-evident, that all men are created equal, that they are endowed by their Creator with certain unalienable rights.' Similarly inspiring sentiments were included in the French *Déclaration des droits de l'homme et du citoyen* of 26 August 1789 which refers to certain 'natural rights' of mankind.

Natural law was applied in the form of a number of contractarian theories that conceive of political rights and obligations in terms of a social contract. It is not a contract in a strict legal sense, but expresses the idea that only with his consent can a person be subjected to the political power of another. This approach remains influential in liberal thought, notably John Rawls's theory of justice (see Chapter 4).

Natural rights: Hobbes, Locke, and Rousseau

Although Thomas Hobbes (1588–1679) is usually remembered for his dictum that life is 'solitary, poor, nasty, brutish and short', he actually said, in his famous work, *Leviathan*, that this was the condition of man before the social contract, i.e. in his natural state. Natural law, he contends, teaches us the necessity of self-preservation: law and government are required if we are to protect order and security. Under the social contract, we must therefore surrender our natural freedom in order to create an orderly society. Hobbes's philosophy is thus somewhat authoritarian, placing order above justice. In particular, his theory (indeed, his self-confessed objective) is to undermine the legitimacy of revolutions against (even malevolent) government.

For Hobbes every act we perform, though ostensibly kind or altruistic, is actually self-serving. Thus my donation to charity is actually a means of enjoying my power. An accurate account of human action, including morality, must, he argues, acknowledge our essential selfishness. In *Leviathan* he wonders how we might behave in a state of nature, before the formation of any government. He recognizes that we are essentially equal, mentally and physically: even the weakest—suitably armed—has the strength to kill the strongest.

This equality, he suggests, generates discord. We tend to wrangle, he argues, for three main reasons: competition (for limited supplies of material possessions); distrust; and glory (we remain hostile in order to preserve our powerful reputations). As a consequence of our propensity toward disagreement, Hobbes concludes that we are in a natural state of perpetual war of all against all, where no morality exists, and all live in constant fear.

Until this state of war comes to an end, all have a right to everything, including another person's life. Hobbes argues that, from human self-interest and social agreement alone, one can derive the same kinds of laws that natural lawyers regard as immutably fixed in nature. In order to escape the horror of the state of nature, Hobbes concludes, peace is the first law of nature.

The second law of nature is that we mutually divest ourselves of certain rights (such as the right to take another person's life) so as to achieve peace. This mutual transferring of rights is a contract and is the basis of moral duty. He is under no illusion that merely concluding this contract can secure peace. Such agreements need to be honoured. This is Hobbes's third law of nature.

He acknowledges that since we are selfish we are likely, out of self-interest, to breach contracts. I may break my agreement not to steal from you when I think I can evade detection. And you are aware of this. The only certain means of avoiding this breakdown in our mutual obligations, he argues, is to grant unlimited power to a political sovereign to punish us if we violate our contracts. And again it is a purely selfish reason (ending the state of nature) that motivates us to agree to the establishment of an authority with the power of sanction. But he insists that only when such a sovereign exists can we arrive at any objective determination of right and wrong.

Hobbes supplements his first three laws of nature with several other substantive ones such as the fourth law (to show gratitude toward those who comply with contracts). He concludes that morality consists entirely of these laws of nature, which are arrived at through the social contract. This is a rather different interpretation of natural rights from that championed by classical natural law. But his account might be styled a modern view of natural rights, one that is premised on the basic right of every person to preserve his own life.

John Locke (1632–1704) portrays life before the social contract as anything but the nightmare described by Hobbes. Locke claims that, before the social contract, life was paradise—save for one important shortcoming: in this state of nature, property was inadequately protected. For Locke, therefore (especially in *Two Treatises of Civil Government*), it was in order to rectify this flaw in an otherwise idyllic natural state that man forfeited, under a social contract, some of his freedom. Suggestive of Aquinas's fundamental postulates, Locke's theory rests on an account of man's rights and obligations under God. It is an intricate attempt to explain the operation of the social contract and its terms. It is revolutionary (Locke accepts the right of the people to overthrow tyranny), and it famously emphasizes the right to own property: God owns the earth and has given it to us to enjoy; there can therefore be no right of property, but by 'mixing' his labour with material objects, the labourer acquires the right to the thing he has created.

Locke's perception of private property strongly influenced the framers of the American constitution. He has therefore been both celebrated and reviled as the progenitor of modern capitalism.

The social contract, in his view, preserved the natural rights to life, liberty, and property, and the enjoyment of private rights: the pursuit of happiness—engendered, in civil society, the common good. Whereas for Hobbes natural rights come first, and natural law is derived from them, Locke derives natural rights from natural law—i.e. from reason. Hobbes discerns a natural right of every person to every thing, Locke argues that our natural right to freedom is constrained by the law of nature and its directive that we should not harm each other in 'life, health, liberty, or possessions'. Locke advocates a limited form of government: the checks and balances among branches of government and the genuine representation in the legislature would, in his view, minimize government and maximize individual liberty.

Natural law plays a less important role than the social contract in the theory of Jean-Jacques Rousseau (1712–78). More metaphysical than Hobbes and Locke, Rousseau's social contract (in his *Social Contract*) is an agreement between the individual and the community by which he becomes part of what Rousseau calls the 'general will'. There are, in Rousseau's view, certain natural rights that cannot be removed, but, by investing the 'general will' with total legislative authority, the law may legitimately infringe upon these rights.

His concept of the general will is tied to his concept of sovereignty which, in his view, is not merely legitimate political power, but its exercise in pursuit of the public good. Thus the general will promotes the interests of the people. Its objective, however, is 'general' in the sense that it can establish rules, social classes, or even a monarchy, but it can never specify the individuals who are subject to the rules, members of the classes, or the rulers. To do so would undermine his essential notion that the general will addresses the good of the society *as a whole* rather than an assembly of individual wills that place their own desires, or those of particular factions, above the needs of the people at large.

His notorious suggestion that man must 'be forced to be free' should be taken to mean that individuals surrender their free will to create popular sovereignty. Moreover, as the indivisible and inalienable 'general will' decides what is best for the community, where an individual lapses into selfishness, he or she must be compelled to fall in line with the dictates of the community.

His idea of the 'general will' is sometimes treated as synonymous with the rule of law; it is a fundamental element of Rousseau's theory of political legitimacy. As long as government represents the 'general will' it may do almost anything. Thus Rousseau, although committed to participatory democracy, is willing to invest the legislature with almost unrestrained power because it represents the 'general will'. He is thus a paradox: a democrat and yet a totalitarian.

But since, in Rousseau's view, the general will is a fool-proof yardstick, it intervenes only when it would be in the interests of society as a whole. It is therefore arguable that his seemingly totalitarian approach is tempered by the importance he attaches to equality and liberty. Legitimate interference by the sovereign might thus be interpreted as required only in order to advance freedom and equality, not to diminish them. The balance between the absolute power of the state and the rights of individuals rests on a social contract that protects society against sectional and class interests.

The fall and rise of natural law

The waning influence of natural law theory, especially in the 19th century, resulted from the emergence of two formidable foes. First, as we shall see in the next chapter, the ideas associated with legal positivism constitute resilient opposition to natural law thinking. Second, the idea that in moral reasoning there can be no rational solutions (so-called non-cognitivism in ethics) spawned a profound scepticism about natural law: If we cannot objectively know what is right or wrong, natural law principles are little more than subjective opinion: they could, therefore, be neither right nor wrong.

David Hume (1711–76) in his *Treatise of Human Nature* first observed that moralists seek to derive an 'ought' from an 'is': we cannot conclude that the law should assume a particular form merely because a certain state of affairs exists in nature. Thus the following syllogism, according to this argument, is invalid:

> All animals procreate (major premise)
> Human beings are animals (minor premise)
> Therefore humans *ought* to procreate (conclusion).

Hume sought to show that facts about the world or human nature cannot be used to determine what *ought* to be done or not done. Some contemporary natural lawyers, while admitting that the above syllogism is indeed false, deny that classical natural law attempted to derive an 'ought' from an 'is' in this manner, as we shall see below.

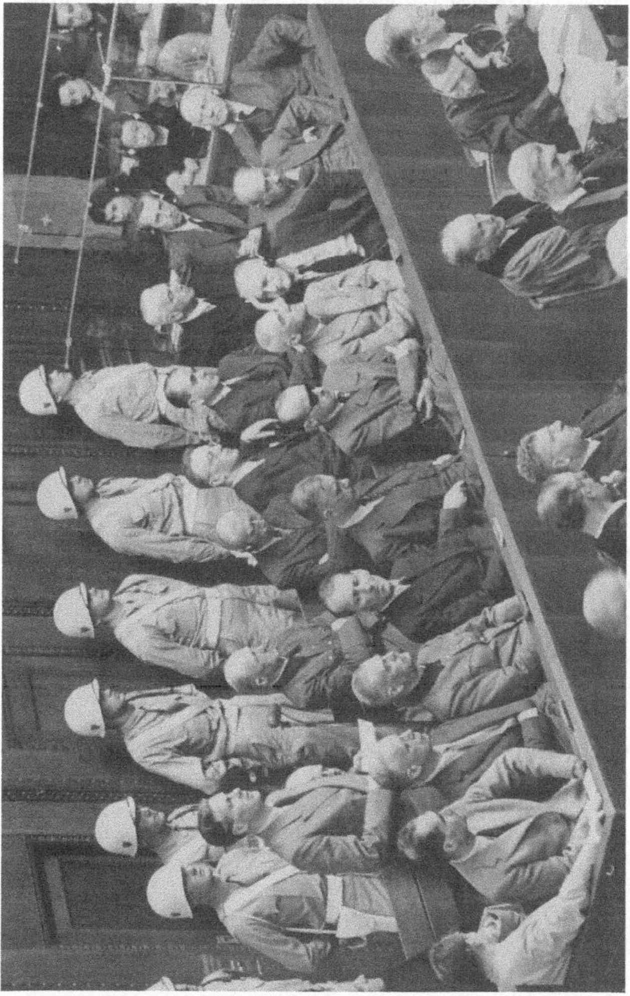

2. The Nuremberg trials of Nazi war criminals applied the principle that certain acts constitute 'crimes against humanity' even though they do not offend against specific provisions of positive law

The 20th century witnessed a renaissance in natural law theory. This is evident in the post-war recognition of human rights and their expression in declarations such as the Charter of the United Nations, and the Universal Declaration of Human Rights, the European Convention on Human Rights, and the Declaration of Delhi on the Rule of Law of 1959 (see Chapter 4). Natural law is conceived of not as a 'higher law' in the constitutional sense of invalidating ordinary law but as a benchmark against which to measure positive law.

The Nuremberg war trials of senior Nazi officials regenerated natural law ideals. They applied the principle that certain acts constitute 'crimes against humanity' even if they do not violate provisions of positive law (Figure 2). The judges in these trials did not appeal explicitly to natural law theory, but their judgments represent an important recognition of the principle that the law is not necessarily the sole determinant of what is right.

Another significant development was the enactment of constitutional safeguards for human or civil rights in various jurisdictions (e.g. the American Bill of Rights and its interpretation by the United States Supreme Court). See Chapter 4.

Legal theory has also advanced the cause of natural law theory. Lon Fuller's 'inner morality of law' (see below), H. L. A. Hart's 'minimum content of natural law' (see Chapter 2), and most importantly, the writings of contemporary natural lawyers such as John Finnis (see below) have played a major role in this revival.

Lon Fuller: the 'inner morality of law'

The American jurist, Lon L. Fuller (1902–78) famously developed a secular natural law approach that regards law as having an 'inner morality'. By this he means that a legal system has the specific purpose of 'subjecting human conduct to the governance of rules'. It follows that in this purposive enterprise there is a necessary connection between law and morality.

Fuller recounts the 'moral' tale of a fictional King Rex and the eight ways in which he fails to make law. He goes wrong because (1) he fails to achieve rules at all, so that every issue must be decided on an ad hoc basis; (2) he does not publicize the rules that his subjects are expected to observe; (3) he abuses his legislative powers by enacting retroactive legislation (i.e. on Tuesday making unlawful those acts that were lawful on Monday); (4) his rules are incomprehensible; (5) he enacts contradictory rules or (6) rules that require conduct beyond the powers of the affected party; (7) he introduces such frequent changes in the rules that his subjects cannot adjust their action; and (8) he fails to achieve congruence between the rules as announced and their actual administration.

Ill-fated King Rex bites the dust because he disregards Fuller's eight principles:

1. Generality
2. Promulgation
3. Non-retroactivity
4. Clarity
5. Non-contradiction
6. Possibility of compliance
7. Constancy
8. Congruence between declared rule and official action.

Fuller concludes that where a system does not conform to any one of these principles, or fails substantially in respect of several, it could not be said that 'law' existed in that community. But, though he insists that these eight principles are *moral*, they appear to be essentially procedural guides to effective lawmaking. Some, however, would argue that they implicitly establish fairness between the government and the governed and therefore exclude evil regimes.

3. The legal enforcement of racial segregation and discrimination reached its high-water mark in apartheid South Africa

The general view, however, is that compliance with Fuller's eight 'desiderata' certifies only that the legal system functions effectively, and hence, since this cannot be a moral criterion, an evil regime might just as easily satisfy the test. Indeed, it is arguable that, in pursuit of efficacy, a wicked legal system might actually *seek* to fulfil Fuller's principles. Certainly, the rulers of apartheid South Africa sought to comply with procedural niceties when enacting and implementing its obnoxious laws (Figure 3).

Contemporary natural law theory: John Finnis

The Aquinian tenets of natural law have been revived and meticulously explored by the Oxford legal theorist, John Finnis

(b. 1940), most accessibly and comprehensively in his book, *Natural Law and Natural Rights*. It represents a significant restatement of classical natural law doctrine, especially its application of analytical jurisprudence to a theory that, as we shall see, is normally regarded as its opposite.

It is important to grasp the purpose of Finnis's enterprise. He rejects David Hume's conception of practical reason, which maintains that my reason for undertaking an action is merely ancillary to my desire to attain a certain objective. Reason informs me only how best to achieve my desires; it cannot tell me what I ought to desire. Finnis prefers an Aristotelian foundation: what constitutes a worthwhile, valuable, desirable life? And his menu contains what he calls the seven 'basic forms of human flourishing':

1. Life
2. Knowledge
3. Play
4. Aesthetic experience
5. Sociability (friendship)
6. Practical reasonableness
7. 'Religion'

These are the essential features that contribute to a fulfilling life. Each is universal in that it governs all human societies at all times, and each has intrinsic value in that it should be valued for its own sake and not merely to achieve some other good. The purpose of moral beliefs is to provide an ethical structure to the pursuit of these basic goods. These principles facilitate our choosing among competing goods and enable us to define what we are permitted to do in pursuing a basic good.

To flourish as human beings, we require these basic goods, though one could easily add to this list. Note that by 'religion', Finnis does not mean organized religion, but the need for spiritual experience.

These seven basic goods are combined by Finnis with the following nine 'basic requirements of practical reasonableness':

1. The active pursuit of goods
2. A coherent plan of life
3. No arbitrary preference among values
4. No arbitrary preference among persons
5. Detachment and commitment
6. The (limited) relevance of consequences: efficiency within reason
7. Respect for every basic value in every act
8. The requirements of the common good
9. Following one's conscience.

These two inventories together comprise the universal and immutable 'principles of natural law'. Finnis demonstrates that this position accords with the general conception of natural law espoused by Thomas Aquinas. Nor, he claims, does it fall victim to non-cognitivist attack by Hume (see above)—for these objective goods are *self-evident*; they are not deduced from any account of human nature. So, for example, 'knowledge' is self-evidently preferable to ignorance. And even if I refute this view, and claim that 'ignorance is bliss', I would willy-nilly be acknowledging that my argument is a valuable one, and hence that knowledge is indeed good, thereby slipping into the trap of self-refutation!

The overriding rationale of natural law theory thus seems to be, as Finnis says, to establish 'what is really good for human persons'. We cannot pursue human goods until we have a community. And the authority of a leader derives from his serving the best interests of that community. Hence, should he enact unjust laws, because they militate against the common good, they would lack the direct moral authority to bind.

Appealing to the concept of the common good, Finnis develops also his conception of justice. Principles of justice, he contends, are no more than the implications of the general requirement that one ought to foster the common good in one's community. The basic goods and methodological requirements ought to thwart most forms of injustice; they generate several absolute obligations with correlative absolute natural rights:

> There is, I think, no alternative but to hold in one's mind's eye some pattern, or range of patterns, of human character, conduct, and interaction in community, and then to choose such specification of rights as tends to favour the pattern, or range of patterns. In other words, *one needs some conception of human good, of individual flourishing in a form (or range of forms) of communal life that fosters rather than hinders such flourishing*. One attends not merely to character types desirable in the abstract or in isolation, but also to the quality of interaction among persons; and one should not seek to realize some patterned 'end-state' imagined in abstraction from the processes of individual initiative and interaction, processes which are integral to human good and which make the future, let alone its evaluation, incalculable.

This passage captures the spirit of Finnis's conception of natural rights. It includes the right not to be tortured, not to have one's life taken as a means to any further end, not to be lied to, not to be condemned on knowingly false charges, not to be deprived of one's capacity to procreate, and the right 'to be taken into respectful consideration in any assessment of what the common good requires'. The concept of justice is further examined in Chapter 4.

Finnis insists that the first principles of natural law are *not* deductively inferred from anything at all, including facts, speculative principles, metaphysical propositions about human nature or about the nature of good and evil, or from a teleological conception of nature. Aquinas, according to Finnis, makes it clear that each of us 'by experiencing one's nature, so to speak, from the inside' grasps 'by a simple act of non-inferential understanding' that 'the object of the inclination which one experiences is an instance of a general form of good, for oneself (and others like one)'. For Aquinas, to discover what is morally right is to ask, not what is in accordance with human nature, but what is *reasonable*.

Moral dilemmas: abortion and euthanasia

These are, quite literally, life and death questions that pose difficult challenges to both morality and law. The subject of abortion is highly contentious—especially in the United States. On the one hand, Christian groups condemn (occasionally violently) the practice as the murder of a potential human being. On the other hand, feminists, among others, regard the matter as fundamental to a woman's right to control her own body. There is no obvious middle ground. Ronald Dworkin vividly describes the intensity and acrimony of the skirmish:

> The war between anti-abortion groups and their opponents is America's new version of the terrible 17th-century European civil wars of religion. Opposing armies march down streets or pack themselves into protests at abortion clinics, courthouses, and the White House, screaming at and spitting on and loathing one another. Abortion is tearing America apart.

At the core of the controversy is the 1973 legendary decision of the United States Supreme Court decision in *Roe* v *Wade*. The judges decided that the abortion law of Texas which criminalized abortion, except when performed to save the pregnant woman's life, was unconstitutional as a violation of the right to privacy. The judgment established the right of states to prohibit abortion to protect the life of the foetus only in the third trimester. The ambition of many Christian groups is to see the judgment overruled. It is a delicate thread by which the right of American women to a lawful abortion hangs.

Somehow the sanctity of human life has to be morally evaluated against the right of a woman over her body. Most European countries have sought to strike this balance by legislation that permits abortion within specified periods under certain prescribed conditions.

In pursuit of a just resolution to this complex subject each society needs to consider its own moral norms. If human life is sacred, does a foetus count as a person capable of suffering harm? If so, how is ending its life to be distinguished from the humane killing of a living human? Should the welfare of the as yet unborn prevail over the distress suffered by a woman compelled to bear an unwanted pregnancy or endure the anxiety, cost, and difficulty of bringing up a severely disabled child?

Similar difficulties inexorably arise in regard to the subject of euthanasia. Doctors, lawyers, and eventually judges increasingly encounter the contentious question of an individual's 'right to die'. A distinction is often drawn (not always convincingly) between active and passive euthanasia. The former entails the acceleration of a person's life by a positive act, such as an injection of potassium chloride. Most legal systems treat this as murder. The latter involves the curbing of life by an omission to act: a withdrawal of treatment, which is increasingly accepted as humane by both the law and the medical profession in many jurisdictions. But courts have not always found it easy to determine the lawfulness of withdrawing life support from an incurably or terminally ill patient who is in a persistent vegetative state (PVS), unable to make an autonomous decision.

Generalities are not easy in respect of either the morality or lawfulness of ending the life of a patient. There is, for example, an important difference between a patient who is incurable, and one who is terminally ill. And in the case of the latter, there is a continuum ranging from incapacity (a fully conscious patient who can breathe unaided), artificial support (a fully conscious patient attached to a ventilator), unconsciousness, to intensive care (where the patient is comatose and is attached to a ventilator). Different factors arise in each of these cases.

The intricate distinctions generated when the law confronts intractable moral questions of this kind suggest that they are not susceptible to resolution by slogans such as 'the right to die', 'autonomy', 'self-determination', or 'the sanctity of life'. Courts may not be the most appropriate arbiters in these circumstances, but is there a realistic alternative? Two decisions of the courts (one English, the other American) illustrate how difficult these problems are in practice.

The English case arose out of an accident that occurred at a crowded football stadium in 1989. Anthony Bland sustained hypoxic brain damage which left him in a persistent vegetative state. Though his brain stem continued to function, his cerebral cortex (the seat of consciousness, communicative activity, and voluntary movement) was destroyed through lack of oxygen, but he was not 'legally dead'. The judge described his wretched state as follows:

> He lies in ... hospital ... fed liquid food by a pump through a tube passing through his nose and down the back of his throat into his stomach. His bladder is emptied through a catheter inserted through his penis, which from time to time has caused infections requiring dressing and antibiotic treatment. His stiffened joints have caused his limbs to be rigidly contracted so that his arms are tightly flexed across his chest and his legs unnaturally contorted. Reflex movements in his throat cause him to vomit and dribble. Of all of this, and the presence of members of his family who take turns to visit him, Anthony Bland has no consciousness at all ... The darkness and oblivion ... will never depart.

His prognosis was not encouraging: his terrible condition could endure for a long time. His doctors applied to the court for permission to withdraw his ventilation, antibiotic, and artificial feeding and hydration regime, while continuing otherwise to treat him so as to allow him to die with dignity, and minimal pain and suffering. The Official Solicitor (who acts for those under a disability) maintained that this would constitute a breach of the doctor's duty to the patient, and a criminal offence.

The court gave priority to the right of self-determination over the right to life. A doctor, it held, should respect his or her patient's rights in that order. This, the judges said, is especially persuasive where the patient has, in anticipation of his or her succumbing to a condition such as PVS, expressed his or her clear wish not to be given medical care, including artificial feeding, calculated to keep him or her alive. But, though all five judges agreed that Bland's life should be allowed to end, there is no clear consensus among their judgments in respect of precisely what the law was or should be. All recognized both the sanctity of life and the autonomy of the patient, but what remained unanswered was how these values were to be reconciled in the absence of an explicit expression of instructions by Bland.

Similar cases have been heard by several courts in the United States and Canada. In the well-known decision of the United States Supreme Court of *Cruzan*, for instance (involving a patient in a PVS whose parents sought to persuade the court that, though she had not expressed this in a 'living will', their daughter would not have wanted to continue living), it was held that the state had an interest in the sanctity, and hence, the preservation of life. The state's interest in preserving life looms large in the judgments.

The court decided that the withdrawal of Bland's nutrition and hydration did not constitute a criminal offence because any hope of his recovery had been abandoned, and, although the termination of his life was not in his best interests neither was his being kept alive. There was no justification, the judges held, for the non-consensual regime and the duty to maintain it. In the absence of this duty, the withdrawal of nutrition and hydration was not a criminal offence.

Courts cannot escape these agonizing quandaries. Their burden is, however, significantly alleviated by the existence of a 'living will' in which an individual stipulates that, for example, 'If, as a result of physical or mental incapacity, I become unable to participate in decisions concerning my medical care and treatment, and subsequently develop any of the medical conditions described below (from which two independent physicians certify I have no reasonable prospect of recovering), I declare that my life should not be sustained by artificial means.'

The central claims of natural law are rejected by legal positivists who deny that that the legal validity of a norm *necessarily* depends on its substantive moral qualities. This standpoint is considered in the next chapter.

Chapter 2
Legal positivism

Imagine a powerful sovereign who issues commands to his or her subjects. They are under a duty to comply with his or her wishes. The notion of law as a command lies at the heart of classical legal positivism as espoused by its two great protagonists, Jeremy Bentham and John Austin. Modern legal positivists adopt a considerably more sophisticated approach to the concept of law, but, like their distinguished predecessors, they deny the relationship proposed by natural law, outlined in the previous chapter, between law and morals. The claim of natural lawyers that law consists of a series of propositions derived from nature through a process of reasoning is strongly contested by legal positivists. This chapter describes the essential elements of this important approach to law and morals, and their relationship to each other.

The term 'positivism' derives from the Latin *positum*, which refers to the law as it is laid down or posited. Broadly speaking, the core of legal positivism is the view that the validity of any law can be traced to an objectively verifiable source. Put simply, legal positivism, like scientific positivism, rejects the view—held by natural lawyers—that law exists independently from human enactment. As will become clear in this chapter, the early legal positivism of Bentham and Austin found the origin of law in the command of a sovereign. H. L. A. Hart looks to a rule of recognition that distinguishes law from other social rules. Hans Kelsen identifies a basic norm that validates the constitution. Legal positivists also often claim that there is no necessary connection between law and morals, and that the analysis of legal concepts is worth pursuing, and distinct from (though not hostile to) sociological and historical enquiries and critical evaluation.

The highest common factor among legal positivists is that the law as laid down should be kept separate—for the purpose of study and analysis—from the law as it ought morally to be. In other words, that a clear distinction must be drawn between 'ought' (that which is morally desirable) and 'is' (that which actually exists). But it does not follow from this that a legal positivist is indifferent to moral questions. Most legal positivists criticize the law and propose means to reform it. This normally involves moral judgements. But positivists do share the view that the most effective method of analysing and understanding law involves suspending moral judgement until it is established what it is we are seeking to elucidate.

Nor do positivists necessarily subscribe to the proposition, often ascribed to them, that unjust or iniquitous laws must be obeyed—merely because they are law. Indeed, both Austin and Bentham acknowledge that disobedience to evil laws is legitimate if it would promote change for the good. In the words of the foremost modern legal positivist H. L. A. Hart:

> [T]he certification of something as legally valid is not conclusive of the question of obedience, ... [H]owever great the aura of majesty or authority which the official system may have, its demands must in the end be submitted to a moral scrutiny.

For Hart, as well as Bentham, this is one of the major virtues of legal positivism.

Law as commands: Bentham and Austin

The prodigious writings of Jeremy Bentham (1748–1832) constitute a major contribution to positivist jurisprudence and the systematic analysis of law and the legal system. Not only did he seek to expose the shibboleths of his age and construct a comprehensive theory of law, logic, politics, and psychology, founded on the principle of utility, but he essayed for reform of the law on almost every subject. His critique of the common law and its theoretical underpinnings are especially ferocious. Moved by the spirit of the Enlightenment, Bentham sought to subject the common law to the cold light of reason. He attempted to demystify the law, to expose, in his characteristically acerbic style, what lay behind its mask. Appeals to natural law were nothing more than 'private opinion in disguise' or 'the mere opinion of men self-constituted into legislatures' (see Figure 4).

The indeterminacy of the common law, he argued, is endemic. Unwritten law is intrinsically vague and uncertain. It cannot provide a reliable, public standard which can reasonably be expected to guide behaviour. The chaos of the common law had to be dealt with systematically. For Bentham this lay, quite simply, in codification. Legal codes would significantly diminish the power of judges; their task would consist less of interpreting than administering the law. It would also remove much of the need for lawyers: the code would be readily comprehensible without the help of legal advisers. Unlike the Continental system of law that has long adopted Napoleonic codes based on Roman law, codification in the common law world remains a dream.

John Austin (1790–1859) published his major work, *The Province of Jurisprudence Determined*, in 1832, the year of Bentham's death. As a disciple of Bentham's, Austin's conception of law is based on the idea of commands or imperatives, though he provides a less elaborate account of what they are. Both jurists

4. Jeremy Bentham: the Luther of legal philosophy?

stress the subjection of persons by the sovereign to his power, but Austin's definition is sometimes thought to extend not very much further than the criminal law, with its emphasis on control over behaviour. His identification of commands as the hallmark of law leads him to a more restrictive definition of law than is adopted by Bentham who seeks to formulate a single, complete law which sufficiently expresses the legislative will.

However, both share a concern to confine the scope of jurisprudential enquiry to accounting for and explaining the principal features of the law. In the case of Austin, though, his map of 'law properly so called' is considerably narrower than Bentham's, and embraces two categories: the laws of God and human laws. Human laws (i.e. laws set down by men for men) are further divided into positive laws or laws 'strictly so called' (i.e. laws laid down by men as political superiors or in pursuance of legal rights) and laws laid down by men not as political superiors or not in pursuance of legal rights. Laws 'improperly so called' are divided into laws by analogy (e.g. laws of fashion, constitutional, and international law) and by metaphor (e.g. the law of gravity). Laws by analogy, together with laws set by men not as political superiors or in pursuance of legal right, are merely 'positive morality'. It is only positive law that is the proper subject of jurisprudence.

Bentham is best known as a utilitarian (see Chapter 4) and law reformer. But he insisted on the separation between what he called 'expositorial' and 'censorial' jurisprudence. The former describes what is, the latter what ought to be. Austin was no less categorical in preserving this division, but his analysis is narrower in both its compass and purpose than Bentham's.

Though both adhere to a utilitarian morality, and adopt broadly similar views on the nature and function of jurisprudence and the serious inadequacies of the common law tradition, there are several important differences in their general approach to the subject. In particular, as already mentioned, Bentham pursues the notion of a single, complete law which adequately expresses the will of the legislature. He seeks to show how a single law creates a single offence defined by its being the narrowest species of that kind of offence recognized by the law.

Austin, on the other hand, builds his scheme of a legal system on the classification of rights; he is not troubled by a search for a 'complete' law. Also, in his pursuit to provide a plan of a comprehensive body of laws and the elements of the 'art of legislation', Bentham expounds a complex 'logic of the will'. Austin seeks to construct a science of law rather than engage himself in Bentham's art of legislation. And while Bentham sought to devise means by which arbitrary power, especially of judges, might be checked, Austin was less anxious about these matters.

The central feature of Austin's map of the province of jurisprudence is the notion of law as a command of the sovereign. Anything that is not a command is not law. Only general commands count as law. And only commands emanating from the sovereign are 'positive laws'. Austin's insistence on law as commands requires him to exclude customary, constitutional, and public international law from the field of jurisprudence. This is because no specific sovereign can be identified as the author of their rules. Thus, in the case of public international law, sovereign states are notoriously at liberty to disregard its requirements.

For Bentham, however, commands are merely one of four methods by which the sovereign enacts law. He distinguishes between laws which command or prohibit certain conduct (imperative laws) and those which permit certain conduct (permissive laws). He contends that all laws are both penal and civil; even in the case of title to property there is a penal element. Bentham seeks to show that laws which impose no obligations or sanctions (what he calls 'civil laws') are not 'complete laws', but merely parts of laws. And, since his principal objective was the creation of a code of law, he argued that the penal and civil branches should be formulated separately.

The relationship between commands and sanctions is no less important for Austin. Indeed, his very concept of a command includes the probability that a sanction will follow failure to obey the command. But what is a sanction? Austin defines it as some harm, pain, or evil that is conditional upon the failure of a person to comply with the wishes of the sovereign. There must be a

Philosophical taxidermy?

'[F]or every legal positivist who regards his theory of law as therapeutic and progressive, there is a natural lawyer who sees it as desiccated and distorting. According to these critics, legal positivism is . . . a well-intentioned idea taken to absurd extremes. In its zeal to demystify, even shock, it trivializes and transmogrifies. Natural lawyers regard legal positivism as a sort of philosophical taxidermy: it hollows out and drains the law of its moral guts and lifeblood, then [like Bentham's preserved body on show in University College, London] wheels out and displays the stuffed mount as though it were the real thing.'

Scott J. Shapiro, *Legality*, p. 388

realistic probability that it will be inflicted upon anyone who infringes a command. There need only be the *threat* of the possibility of a minimal harm, pain, or evil, but unless a sanction is likely to follow, the mere expression of a wish is not a command. Obligations are therefore defined in terms of sanctions: this is a central tenet of Austin's imperative theory. The likelihood of a sanction is always uncertain, but Austin is driven to the rather unsatisfactory position that a sanction consists of 'the smallest chance of incurring the smallest evil'.

The idea of a sovereign who issues commands pervades the theories of both Bentham and Austin. It is important to note that both regard the sovereign's power as constituted by the habit of the people generally obeying his laws. But while Austin insists on the illimitability and indivisibility of the sovereign, Bentham, alive to the institution of federalism, acknowledges that the supreme legislative power may be both limited and divided by what he calls an express convention.

For Austin, to the four features of a command (wish, sanction, expression of a wish, and generality) is to be added a fifth, namely an identifiable political superior—or sovereign—whose commands are obeyed by political inferiors and who owes obedience to no one. This insistence on an omnipotent lawgiver distorts those legal systems which impose constitutional restrictions on the legislative competence of the legislature or which divide such power between a central federal legislature and lawmaking bodies of constituent states or provinces (such as in the United States, Canada or Australia). Bentham, on the other hand, acknowledges that sovereignty may be limited or divided, and accepts (albeit reluctantly) the possibility of judicial review of legislative action.

Austin's contention that 'laws properly so called' be confined to the commands of a sovereign leads him to base his idea of sovereignty on the habit of obedience adopted by members of society. The sovereign must, moreover, be determinate (i.e. the composition of the sovereign body must be unambiguous), for 'no indeterminate sovereign can command expressly or tacitly, or can receive obedience or submission'. And this results in Austin famously refusing to accept as 'law' public international law, customary law, and a good deal of constitutional law.

Moreover, by insisting that the sanction is an indispensable ingredient in the definition of law, Austin is driven to defining duty in terms of sanction: if the sovereign expresses a wish and has the power to inflict an evil (or sanction) then a person is under a duty to act in accordance with that wish. The distinction between a 'wish' and the 'expression of a wish' resembles the distinction between a bill and a statute.

Austin's association between duty and sanction has attracted considerable criticism, though it may be that he was merely seeking to show—in a formal sense—that, where there is a duty, its breach normally gives rise to a sanction. In other words, he is not necessarily seeking to provide an explanation for why law is obeyed or whether it ought to be obeyed, but rather when a legal duty exists. Nevertheless, he unquestionably accords unwarranted significance to the concept of duty. The law frequently imposes no direct duty, such as when it facilitates marriage, contracts, and wills. We are not under any duty to carry out these transactions, but they are plainly part of the law. H. L. A. Hart calls them 'power-conferring rules' (see later in the chapter).

The less dogmatic approach of Bentham allows that a sovereign's commands constitute law even in the absence of sanctions in the Austinian sense. Law, according to Bentham, includes both punishments ('coercive motives') and rewards ('alluring motives'), but they do not define what is and what is not law.

A sanction is best regarded as some form of disadvantage which involves some loss of a benefit or an extra burden such as a penalty or duty. Bentham rejects this element, and calls a reward a 'praemiary sanction' because it could encourage compliance. Thus Bentham is innocent of the narrow vision of law and the legal system that is an important weakness in Austin's system.

Bentham and Austin laid the foundations for modern legal positivism. But their ideas have been considerably refined, developed, and even rejected, by contemporary legal positivists. The remainder of this chapter outlines the approaches of its three leading protagonists: H. L. A. Hart, Hans Kelsen, and Joseph Raz.

Law as social rules: H. L. A. Hart

H. L. A. Hart (1907–92) is often credited with charting the map of modern legal theory by applying the techniques of analytical, and especially linguistic, philosophy to the study of law (see Figure 5). His work illuminates the meaning of legal concepts, the manner in which we deploy them, and the way we think about law and the legal system. What, for example, does it mean to have a 'right'? What is a corporation or an obligation? Hart claims that we cannot properly understand law unless we understand the

5. H. L. A. Hart: the father of modern legal positivism

conceptual context in which it emerges and develops. He argues, for instance, that language has an 'open texture': words (and hence rules) have a number of clear meanings, but there are always several 'penumbral' cases where it is uncertain whether the word applies or not. His book, *The Concept of Law*, published in 1961, is a classic of legal theory and has served as a catalyst for many other jurists around the world.

Hart's positivism is a far cry from the largely coercive picture of law painted by Bentham and Austin. Hart conceives of law as a social phenomenon that can be understood only by describing the actual social practices of a community. In order for it to survive as a community, Hart argues, there need to be certain fundamental rules. He calls these the 'minimum content of natural law'. They arise out of our human condition which manifests the following essential features:

> 'Human vulnerability': We are all susceptible to physical attacks.
>
> 'Approximate equality': Even the strongest must sleep at times.
>
> 'Limited altruism': We are, in general, selfish.
>
> 'Limited resources': We need food, clothes, and shelter, and they are limited.
>
> 'Limited understanding and strength of will': We cannot be relied upon to cooperate with our fellow men.

These human frailties require the enactment of rules to protect persons and property, and to ensure that promises are kept. But, though he employs the shibboleth 'natural law', he does not mean that law is derived from morals or that there is a necessary conceptual relationship between the two. Nor is he saying that this minimum content of natural law ensures a fair or just society. Hart severs his legal positivism from both the utilitarianism (see Chapter 4) and the command theory of law championed by Austin and Bentham. In the case of the latter, his rejection is based on the view that law is more than the decree of a gunman: a command backed by a sanction.

Marginalized positivists?

'[A]nalytic positivists continue to treat their conceptual investigations of law as independent of both legal substance and political philosophy. But they talk mainly to one another and have become marginalized within the academy and the profession.'

Ronald Dworkin, *Justice in Robes*, p. 34

The nucleus of Hart's theory is the existence of fundamental rules accepted by officials as stipulating procedures by which the law is enacted. The most important of these he calls the rule of recognition which is the fundamental constitutional rule of a legal system, acknowledged by those officials who administer the law as specifying the conditions or criteria of validity which certify whether or not a rule is indeed a rule.

Law, in Hart's analysis, is a system of rules. His argument is as follows. All societies have social rules. These include rules relating to morals, games, etc., as well as obligation rules that impose duties or obligations. The latter may be divided into moral rules and legal rules (or law). As a result of our human limitations, mentioned above, there is a necessity for obligation rules in all societies. Legal rules are divisible into primary rules and secondary rules. The former proscribe the use of violence, theft, and deception to which human beings are tempted but which they must normally repress if they are to coexist in close proximity. The rules of primitive societies are normally restricted to these primary rules imposing obligations.

But as a society becomes more complex, there is obviously a need to change the primary rules, to adjudicate on breaches of them, and to identify which rules are actually obligation rules. These three requirements are satisfied in each case in modern societies by the introduction of three sorts of secondary rules: rules of change, adjudication, and recognition. Unlike primary rules, the first two of these secondary rules do not generally impose duties, but usually confer power. The rule of recognition, however, does seem to impose duties (largely on judges). I expand on this point below.

The existence of a legal system requires that two conditions must be satisfied. First, valid obligation rules must be generally obeyed by members of society, and, second, officials must accept the rules of change and adjudication; they must also accept the rule of recognition 'from the internal point of view'.

As already pointed out, Hart rejects Austin's conception of rules as commands, and the notion that rules are phenomena that consist merely in externally observable activities or habit. Instead he asks us to consider the *social* dimension of rules, namely the manner in which members of a society perceive the rule in question, their attitude towards it. This 'internal' aspect distinguishes between a rule and a mere habit.

Thus, to use his example, chess players, in addition to having similar habits of moving the Queen in the same way, also have a 'critical reflective attitude' to this way of moving it: they each regard it as a *standard* for all who play chess. They exhibit these views in their appraisal of other players, and acknowledge the legitimacy of such criticism when they are themselves subjected to it.

In other words, to grasp the nature of rules we must examine them from the point of view of those who *experience* them, or who pass judgement on them. He also employs the concept of a 'rule' to distinguish between 'being obliged' and 'having an obligation'. When a gunman says, 'Your money or your life?' you are obliged to obey, but, says Hart, you have no 'obligation' to do so—because no rule imposes an obligation on you.

Having described the nature and purpose of primary rules, Hart attempts to show that every legal system incorporates secondary rules of three kinds. The first he calls rules of change. These facilitate legislative or judicial changes to both the primary rules and certain secondary rules (e.g. the rule of adjudication, below). This process of change is regulated by secondary rules that confer power on individuals or groups (e.g. Congress or Parliament) to enact legislation in accordance with certain procedures. Rules of change also confer power on you and me to alter our legal status (e.g. by making contracts, wills, etc.).

Second, there are rules of adjudication that confer authority on individuals, such as judges, to pass judgment mainly in cases of breaches of primary rules. This power is normally associated with a further power to punish the wrongdoer or compel the wrongdoer to pay damages.

Third, there is the rule of recognition which determines the criteria by which the validity of all the rules of a legal system is decided. As pointed out above, unlike the other two types of secondary rules, it appears, in part, to be duty-imposing: it requires those who exercise public power (particularly judges) to follow certain rules. Hart maintains that rules are valid members of the legal system only if they satisfy the criteria laid down by the rule of recognition. Comparing it to the standard metre bar in Paris (the definitive standard by which a metre was once measured), the validity of the rule of recognition cannot be questioned. It is neither valid nor invalid, but is simply accepted as the correct standard.

A legal system exists, according to Hart, only if valid primary rules are obeyed, and officials accept the rules of change and adjudication. In Hart's words:

> The assertion that a legal system exists is . . . a Janus-faced statement looking both to obedience by ordinary citizens and to the acceptance by officials of secondary rules as critical common standards of official behaviour.

You and I, as ordinary members of society, do not need to accept the primary rules or the rule of recognition; it is necessary only that the *officials* do so from 'an internal point of view'. What does this mean? Hart's answer is as follows:

> What is necessary is that there should be a critical reflective attitude to certain patterns of behaviour as a common standard, and that this should display itself in criticism (including self-criticism), demands for conformity, and in acknowledgements that such criticism and demands are justified, all of which find their

characteristic expression in the normative terminology of 'ought', 'must', and 'should', 'right' and 'wrong'.

This 'internal' dimension of rules thus distinguishes social rules from mere group habits. By accepting secondary rules, officials need not approve of them. Judges in an iniquitous legal system may detest the rules they are required to apply, but by accepting them they satisfy Hart's conditions for a legal system to exist.

Hart concedes that where a legal system fails to receive general approval, it would be both morally and politically objectionable. But these moral and political criteria are not identifying characteristics of the notion of 'legal system'. The validity of a legal system is therefore independent from its efficacy. A completely ineffective rule may be a valid one—as long as it emanates from the rule of recognition. But to be a valid rule, the legal system of which the rule is a component must, as a whole, be effective.

Law as norms: Hans Kelsen

Hans Kelsen (1881–1973), in his complex 'pure theory of law', expounds a subtle and profound account of the way in which we should understand law. We should do so, he insists, by conceiving it to be a system of 'oughts' or *norms*. Kelsen does concede that the law consists also of legal acts as determined by these norms. But the essential character of law derives from norms—which include judicial decisions and legal transactions such as contracts and wills. Even the most general norms describe human conduct.

Influenced by the great 18th-century philosopher Immanuel Kant, Kelsen accepts that we can understand objective reality only by the application of certain formal categories like time and space that do not 'exist' in nature: we use them in order to make sense of the world. Similarly, to understand 'the law' we need formal categories, such as the basic norm—or *Grundnorm*—which, as its name suggests, lies at the base of any legal system (see below).

Legal theory, argues Kelsen, is no less a science than physics or chemistry. Thus we need to disinfect the law of the impurities of morality, psychology, sociology, and political theory. He thus propounds a sort of ethical cleansing under which our analysis is directed to the norms of positive law: those 'oughts' that declare that if certain conduct (X) is performed, then a sanction (Y) should be applied by an official to the offender. His 'pure' theory thus excludes that which we cannot objectively know, including law's moral, social, or political functions. Law has but one purpose: the monopolization of force.

Kelsen's concept of a norm entails that something ought to be, or that something ought to happen—in particular, that a person ought to behave in a specific way. Hence both the statement 'the door ought to be closed', and a red traffic light constitute norms. To be valid, however, a norm must be authorized by another norm which, in turn, must be authorized by a higher legal norm in the system. Kelsen is intensely relativistic: he repudiates the idea that there are values 'out there'. For him all norms are relative to the individual or group under consideration.

The promotion of social order is achieved by governments enacting norms that determine whether our conduct is lawful or unlawful. These norms, argues Kelsen, provide sanctions for failure to comply with them. Legal norms therefore differ from other norms in that they prescribe a sanction. A legal system is founded on state coercion; behind its norms is the threat of force. This distinguishes the tax collector from the robber. Both demand your money. Both, in other words, require that you *ought* to pay up. Both exhibit a *subjective* act of will, but only the tax collector's is *objectively* valid. Why? Because, says Kelsen, the subjective meaning of the robber's coercive order is not interpreted as its objective meaning. Why not? Because no basic norm is presupposed according to which one ought to comply with this order. And why not? Because the robber's coercive order lacks the 'lasting effectiveness without which no basic norm is presupposed'.

This demonstrates the essential relationship in Kelsen's theory between validity and effectiveness, which is discussed below.

His model of a legal system is therefore a succession of interconnected norms advancing from the most general 'oughts' (e.g. sanctions ought to be effected in accordance with the constitution) to the most particular or 'concrete' (e.g. Charles is contractually bound to mow Camilla's grass). Each norm in this hierarchical system draws its validity from another higher norm. The validity of all norms is ultimately based on the basic norm.

As the validity of each norm depends on a higher norm whose validity depends in turn on another higher norm, we eventually reach a point of no return. This is the basic norm or *Grundnorm*. All norms emanate from this norm in escalating levels of 'concreteness', including the very constitution of the state. Since, by definition, the validity of the basic norm cannot depend on any other norm, it has to be presupposed. Without this presupposition, Kelsen claims, we cannot understand the legal order. The basic norm exists, but only in the 'juristic consciousness'. It is an assumption that makes possible our comprehension of the legal system by the legal scientist, judge, or lawyer. It is not, however, selected arbitrarily, but by reference to whether the legal order as a whole is 'by and large' effective. Its validity depends on efficacy. In other words, the validity of the basic norm rests, not on another norm or rule of law, but is *assumed*—for the purpose of purity. It is therefore a hypothesis, a wholly formal construct.

The nature of the basic norm is illustrated by Kelsen's religious analogy in which a son is instructed by his father to go to school. To this individual norm, the son replies, 'Why should I go to school?' In other words, he asks why the subjective meaning of his father's act of will is its objective meaning, i.e. a norm binding for him—or, which means the same thing, what is the basis of the validity of this norm. The father responds, 'Because God has commanded that parents be obeyed—that is, God has authorized parents to issue commands to children.' The son retorts, 'Why should one obey the commands of God?' He is, in Kelsenian terms, asking why the subjective meaning of this act of will of God is also its objective meaning—that is, a valid norm or, which amounts to the same thing, what is the basis of the validity of this general norm.

The only possible answer to this is: because, as a believer, one presupposes that one ought to obey the commands of God. This is the statement of the validity of a norm that must be presupposed in a believer's thinking in order to ground the validity of the norms of a religious morality. It constitutes the basic norm of a religious morality, the norm that grounds the validity of all the norms of that morality—a 'basic' norm, because no further question can be raised about the basis of its validity. The statement is not a positive norm—i.e. not a norm posited by a real act of will—but a norm presupposed in a believer's thinking.

The basic norm is intended to have two major functions. First, it assists us in distinguishing between the demands of a robber and those of the law. In other words, it enables us to regard a coercive order as objectively valid. Second, it explains the coherence and unity of a legal order. All valid legal norms may be interpreted as a non-contradictory field of meaning.

Kelsen frames the basic norm as follows:

> Coercive acts ought to be performed under the conditions and in the manner which the historically first constitution, and the norms created according to it, prescribe. (In short: One ought to behave as the constitution prescribes.)

The basic norm, as a purely formal construct, has no specific content. Any human conduct, Kelsen says, may be the subject matter of a legal norm. Nor can the validity of a positive legal order be denied merely because of the content of its norms.

Since Kelsen argues that the effectiveness of the whole legal order is a necessary condition of its validity of every norm within it, implicit in the very existence of a legal system is the fact that its laws are generally obeyed. In *The Pure Theory of Law* he puts the matter bluntly: 'Every by and large effective coercive order can be interpreted as an objectively valid normative order.' But this is problematic. How can we know whether laws are actually being observed or disregarded? How do we test whether the law is, in Kelsen's phrase, 'by and large' effective? Many would say that the efficacy or otherwise of a legal order is an empirical matter, something we can witness or observe. But the pure theory spurns 'sociological' enquiries of this kind.

Kelsen also eschews any consideration of the reasons why the law might be effective (its rationality, goodness, etc.). If the validity of a legal order requires the effectiveness of its basic norm, it follows that when that basic norm of the system no longer attracts general support, there is no law. This is what happens after a successful revolution. The existing basic norm no longer exists, and, Kelsen says, once the new laws of the revolutionary government are effectively enforced, lawyers may presuppose a new basic norm. This is because the basic norm is not the constitution, but the presumption that the altered state of affairs ought to be accepted in fact.

Kelsen's ideas have been cited by a number of courts in countries which have experienced revolutions: Pakistan, Uganda, Rhodesia, and Grenada.

Law as social fact: Joseph Raz

The writing of the Oxford philosopher, Joseph Raz (b. 1939) does not lend itself to simple synopsis. As a leading 'hard' or 'exclusivist' legal positivist, Raz maintains that the identity and existence of a legal system may be tested by reference to three elements; efficacy, institutional character, and sources. Law is thus drained of its moral content, based on the idea that legality does not depend on its moral merit. 'Soft' positivists, like H. L. A. Hart, reject this view, and acknowledge that content or merit may be included or incorporated as a condition of validity. They are therefore also called 'incorporationists'.

Raz argues, however, that the law is autonomous: we can identify its content without recourse to morality. Legal *reasoning*, on the other hand, is not autonomous; it is an inevitable, and desirable, feature of judicial reasoning. For Raz, the existence and content of every law may be determined by a *factual* enquiry about conventions, institutions, and the intentions of participants in the legal system. The answer to the question 'what is law?' is always a fact. It is never a moral judgement. This marks him as a 'hard' or 'exclusive' positivist. 'Exclusive' because the reason we regard the law as authoritative is the fact that it is able to guide our behaviour in a way that morality cannot do. In other words, the law asserts its primacy over all other codes of conduct. Law is the ultimate source of authority. Thus, a legal system is quintessentially one of authoritative rules. It is this claim of authority that is the trademark of a legal system.

Raz identifies three principal claims made by positivists and attacked by natural lawyers:

> The 'social thesis': that law may be identified as a social fact, without reference to moral considerations.
>
> The 'moral thesis': that the moral merit of law is neither absolute nor inherent, but contingent upon 'the content of the law and the circumstances of the society to which it applies'.
>
> The 'semantic thesis': that normative terms such as 'right' and 'duty' are not used in moral and legal contexts in the same way.

Raz accepts only the 'social thesis' on the basis of the three accepted criteria by which a legal system may be identified: its efficacy, its institutional character, and its sources. From all three, moral questions are excluded. Thus, the institutional character of law means simply that laws are identified by their relationship to certain institutions (e.g. the legislature). Anything—however morally acceptable—not admitted by such institutions is not law, and vice versa.

Raz actually postulates a stronger version of the 'social thesis' (the 'sources thesis') as a central feature of legal positivism. His major justification for the sources thesis is that it accounts for a primary function of law: the setting of standards by which we are bound, in such a way that we cannot excuse our non-compliance by challenging the rationale for the standard.

It is mainly upon his acceptance of the social thesis, and his rejection of the moral and semantic theses, that Raz assembles his case against a general moral obligation to obey the law. In reaching this conclusion, he repudiates three common arguments made for the moral authority of law. First, it is often argued that to distinguish, as positivists do, between law and other forms of social control, is to neglect the functions of law; and because functions cannot be described in a value-free manner, any functional account of law must involve moral judgments—and so offend the social thesis. Raz argues that, while law does indeed have certain functions, his own analysis of them is value-neutral.

Nor, second, does Raz accept that the content of law cannot be determined exclusively by social facts: so, for example, since courts unavoidably rely on explicitly moral considerations, they creep into determinations of what the law actually is. Although Raz concedes that moral concerns do enter into adjudication, he insists that this is inevitable in any source-based system. But it does not, in his view, establish a case against the sources thesis. Finally, it is occasionally argued that what is distinctive about the law is that it conforms to the ideal of the rule of law, the belief that no one is above the law. Surely, some contend, this demonstrates that the law is indeed moral. Raz attempts to refute this proposition by arguing that, while conformity to the rule of law reduces the abuse of executive power, it does not confer an independent moral merit upon the law. For him the rule of law is a negative virtue—for the risk of arbitrary power is created by the law itself. He thus concludes that, even in a legal system that is fair and just, there is no prima facie duty to obey the law.

Scott Shapiro has recently postulated a different, highly original positivist account of the nature of law that he calls the 'Planning Theory of Law'. He attempts to show that legal activity is a form of social planning. Legal rules are fundamentally 'generalized plans' or 'planlike norms' for a community originating from legal institutions vested with the authority to issue such plans. Stripped of moral considerations, the fundamental purpose of planning is to obviate or resolve moral problems that beset social life.

Life itself, he contends, is an exercise in planning, whether it be our preparations for cooking dinner or the arrangements we make for our future. The very creation and tenacity of rules of law are based upon the capacity of all individuals to make and execute plans which need not be 'good'. Even a bad plan is a plan which can engender the structure of hierarchy, authority, and institutional complexity that are the hallmarks of law. But, we may ask, is all law really plan-like? Does organizing a society really resemble preparing dinner?

Contemporary legal positivism has grown increasingly technical and sophisticated. A split has developed between so-called hard and soft positivists. The former (who are often described as 'exclusive legal positivists') maintain that all criteria of legality must be 'social sources'. This means that the determination of whether something is 'law' cannot turn on a norm's content or substantive value or merit. The existence of a particular 'law', in other words, does not depend on whether it ought to be the law. Soft positivists (or 'inclusive positivists' or 'incorporationists'), on the other hand, accept that some principles may be legally binding by virtue of their value or merit, but morality can be a condition of validity *only where the rule of recognition so stipulates.*

A soft positivist accepts that the rule of recognition may incorporate moral criteria (hence their often being dubbed 'incorporationists'). Therefore what the law is may sometimes rest on moral considerations. For example, where a constitution (or a bill of rights) requires a court to decide a case by reference to considerations of justice and fairness, he or she will be expected to determine the outcome by evaluating these moral values. Adjudication is therefore no longer confined to the exclusive application of *legal* rules. Hard positivists insist that the validity of a purported legal norm (its membership in the legal system) cannot turn on the moral merits of the norm in question. They therefore acknowledge that occasionally the law may incorporate moral criteria for ascertaining what the law is. In his 'postscript' to *The Concept of Law*, Hart himself seems to have gone soft by accepting that the rule of recognition may incorporate as criteria of legal validity conformity with moral principles. In other words, moral issues seep into the process of determining what is 'law'.

This concession has, not surprisingly, been condemned by hard positivists who claim that these moral standards cannot be applied by a judge as law, for this would amount to a judge having the power to decide whether to apply norms according to his evaluation of their moral worth. But can legal positivism—hard or soft—withstand the attack by its most powerful detractor, Ronald Dworkin, whose legal theory is the subject of the following chapter.

Law and values

'The fear is that ... reference to value deprives legal theory ... of any pretensions to scientific character. Were this true, law schools, so far as they are anything more than trade schools teaching skills and tricks of a sometimes questionable kind of job, would be purveyors of ideology, not disseminators of knowledge and learning. Were it true, jurisprudence would become, or be seen as what it has been all along, an exercise in legitimation of the actual state and its mode of government. Were it true, law professors would be mere apologists for the established order of things, interpreting that in the most attractive possible light ... [H]uman artefacts and contrivances, including any rules by which people try to live, or get others to live, have to be understood functionally. What is their point, what is the final cause to which they are oriented? ... Failure to confront and account openly for values involved, and to defend one's own proposals as to what the relevant values are, may confer work about law an apparently greater objectivity than if a proper openness were practised. But it is the concealment of value-orientation, not its open avowal, that is ideological in a sinister sense. Honest interpretation that is open about the values it presupposes and that is as alert to system-failures as to system-successes judges against those values is the best objectivity that is available to the human sciences, jurisprudence included.'

Neil MacCormick, *Institutions of Law: An Essay in Legal Theory*, p. 305

Chapter 3
Dwarkin: the moral integrity of law

Ronald Dworkin (1931–2013) is legal positivism's most tenacious critic. 'Law', he insisted, 'is effectively integrated with morality: lawyers and judges are working political philosophers of a democratic state.' His long crusade in support of 'the unity of value' began with an assault on legal positivism and, in particular, Hart's version of it, but his theory is considerably wider. It includes not only a stimulating account of law and the legal system, but also an analysis of the place of morals in law, the importance of individual rights, and the nature of the judicial function. And all these elements are skilfully integrated into a single vision of law that seeks to 'take rights seriously'. Moreover, his ideas have sparked a huge critical literature that shows little sign of abating.

He shook the foundations of legal philosophy in the 1970s when Dworkin succeeded H. L. A. Hart as Professor of Jurisprudence at Oxford. The dominance of legal positivism, especially in Britain, was over the next four decades subjected to a comprehensive onslaught in the form of a subtle theory of law that is both controversial and powerful. His ideas continue to exert considerable authority, especially in the United States, whenever contentious moral and political issues are debated. No serious analysis of, say, the role of the United States Supreme Court, the issue of abortion, or general questions of liberty and equality can ignore his views. His constructive vision of law is both a profound

6. Ronald Dworkin regarded law as an interpretive process under which individual rights are paramount

analysis of the concept of law and a compelling entreaty in support of its enrichment.

Among the numerous elements of his sophisticated philosophy is the contention that the law contains a solution to almost every problem. This is at variance with the traditional—positivist—perception that, when a judge is faced with a difficult case to which no statute or previous decision applies, he or she exercises discretion and decides the case on the basis of what seems to him or her to be the correct answer. Dworkin contests this position, and shows how a judge does not make law, but rather *interprets* what is already part of the legal materials. Through an interpretation of these materials, he or she gives voice to the values to which the legal system is committed (see Figure 6).

To understand Dworkin's key proposition that law is a 'gapless' system, consider the following two situations:

> An impatient beneficiary under a will murders the testator. Should he be permitted to inherit?
>
> A chess grand master distracts his opponent by continually smiling at him. The opponent objects. Is smiling in breach of the rules of chess?

Hard cases

These are both 'hard cases' for in neither case is there a determinable rule to resolve it. This gives legal positivists a headache, for, as discussed in the last chapter, positivism generally claims that law consists of rules determined by social facts. Where, as in these examples, rules run out, the problem can be resolved only by the exercise of a subjective, and hence potentially arbitrary, discretion: a lawyer's nightmare.

If, however, there is more to law than rules, as Dworkin claims, then an answer may be found in the law itself. Hard cases such as these may, in other words, be decided by reference to the legal materials; there is no need to reach outside the law and so to allow subjective judgements to enter.

The first puzzle mentioned above is drawn from the New York decision of *Riggs v. Palmer* in 1899. The will in question was validly executed and was in the murderer's favour. But whether a murderer could inherit was uncertain: the rules of testamentary succession provided no applicable exception. The murderer should therefore have a right to his or her inheritance. The New York court held, however, that the application of the rules was subject to the principle that 'no person should profit from his own wrong'. Hence a murderer could not inherit from his or her victim. This decision reveals, Dworkin argues, that, in addition to rules, the law includes *principles*.

In the second dilemma, Dworkin argues, the referee is called upon to determine whether smiling is in breach of the rules of chess. The rules are silent. He or she must therefore consider the nature of chess as a game of intellectual skill; does this include the use of psychological intimidation? He or she must, in other words, find the answer that best 'fits' and explains the practice of chess. To this question there will be a right answer. And this is equally true of the judge deciding a hard case.

Legal systems characteristically generate controversial or hard cases such as these in which a judge may need to consider whether to look beyond the strict letter of what the law is to determine what it ought to be. He or she engages, in other words, in a process of interpretation in which arguments that resemble moral claims feature. This interpretive dimension of law is a fundamental component of Dworkin's theory. His assault on legal positivism is premised on the impossibility of the separation between law and morals that it proposes.

Thus for Dworkin, law consists not merely of rules, as Hart contends, but includes what Dworkin calls non-rule standards. When a court has to decide a hard case it will draw on these (moral or political) standards—principles and policies—in order to reach a decision. No rule of recognition—as described by Hart and discussed in the last chapter—exists to distinguish between legal and moral principles. Deciding what the law is depends inescapably on moral-political considerations.

There are two phases in Dworkin's conception of legal reasoning. First, he contended in the 1970s that legal positivism is unable to explain the significance of legal principles in determining what the law is. In the 1980s, Dworkin advanced a more radical thesis that law was essentially an interpretive phenomenon. This view rests on two main premises. The first maintains that determining what the law requires in a particular case necessarily involves a form of interpretative reasoning. Thus, for example, to claim that the law protects my right of privacy against the *Daily Rumour* constitutes a conclusion of a certain interpretation. The second premise is that interpretation always entails evaluation. If correct, this would all but sound the death knell for legal positivists' separation thesis.

In a hard case the judge therefore draws on principles, including his or her own conception of the best interpretation of the system of political institutions and decisions of the community. 'Could my decision', he or she must ask, 'form part of the best moral theory justifying the whole legal and political system?' There can only be one right answer to every legal problem; the judge has a duty to find it. His or her answer is 'right' in the sense that it fits best with the institutional and constitutional history of his or her society and is morally justified. Legal argument and analysis are therefore 'interpretive' because they attempt to make the best moral sense of legal practices.

Dworkin's attack on legal positivism is crucially founded on his concern that the law ought to 'take rights seriously'. Rights trump other considerations such as community welfare. Individual rights are seriously compromised if, as Hart claims, the result of a hard case depends on the judge's personal opinion, intuition, or the exercise of his or her strong discretion. My rights may then simply be subordinated to the interests of the community. Instead, Dworkin contends, my rights should be recognized as *part of the law*. His theory thus provides more muscle to the defence of individual rights and liberty than legal positivism can deliver.

In his best-known and most comprehensive work, *Law's Empire*, Dworkin launches a wholesale attack on both 'conventionalism' and pragmatism. The former argues that law is a function of social convention which it then designates as legal convention. In other words, it claims that law consists in no more than following certain conventions (e.g. that decisions of higher courts are binding on lower ones). Conventionalism also regards law as incomplete: the law contains 'gaps' which judges fill with their own preferences. Judges, in other words, exercise a 'strong discretion'.

Conventionalist accounts of law, Dworkin argues, fail to provide either a convincing account of the process of lawmaking or an adequately robust defence of individual rights. In Dworkin's vision of 'law as integrity' (see later), a judge must think of him- or herself not, as the conventionalist would claim, as giving voice to his or her own moral or political convictions, or even to those convictions which he or she thinks the legislature or the majority of the electorate would approve, but as an author in a chain of the common law. As Dworkin says,

> He knows that other judges have decided cases that, although not exactly like his case, deal with related problems; he must think of their decisions as part of a long story he must interpret and then continue, according to his own judgment of how to make the developing story as good as it can be.

Pragmatists, according to Dworkin, adopt a sceptical attitude towards the view that past political decisions justify state coercion. Instead, they find such justification in the justice or efficiency or other virtue of the exercise of such coercion by a judge. This approach fails to take rights seriously because it treats rights instrumentally—they have no independent existence: rights are simply a means by which to make life better. Pragmatism rests on the claim that judges do—and should—make whatever decisions seem to them best for the community's future, rejecting consistency with the past as valuable for its own sake.

It is only what Dworkin calls 'law as integrity' (see later) that provides an acceptable justification for the state's use of force. Law's empire, he tells us, 'is defined by attitude, not territory or power or process'. Law, in other words, is an interpretive concept addressed to politics in its widest sense. It adopts a constructive approach in that it seeks to improve our lives and our community.

Principles and policies

Dworkin's account of the judicial function requires the judge to treat the law as if it were a seamless web. There is no law beyond the law. Nor, contrary to the positivist thesis, are there any gaps in the law. Law and morals are inextricably intertwined. There cannot therefore be a rule of recognition, as described in the last chapter, by which to identify the law. Nor does Hart's view of law as a union of primary and secondary rules provide an accurate model, for it omits or at least neglects the importance of principles and policies.

Dworkin claims that, while rules 'are applicable in an all-or-nothing fashion', principles and policies have 'the dimension of weight or importance'. In other words, if a rule applies, and it is a valid rule, a case must be decided in a way dictated by the rule. A principle, on the other hand, provides a reason for deciding the case in a particular way, but it is not a conclusive reason: it will have to be weighed against other principles in the system.

Principles differ from policies in that the former is 'a standard to be observed, not because it will advance or secure an economic, political, or social situation, but because it is a requirement of justice or fairness or some other dimension of morality'. A 'policy', however, is 'that kind of standard that sets out a goal to be reached, generally an improvement in some economic, political, or social feature of the community'.

Principles describe rights; policies describe goals. But rights are trumps. They have a 'threshold weight' against community goals.

They should not be squashed by a competing community goal. Every civil case, he argues, raises the question, 'Does the plaintiff have a right to win?' The community's interests should not come into play. Thus civil cases are, and should be, decided by principles. Even where a judge appears to be advancing an argument of policy, we should interpret him or her as referring to principle because he or she is, in fact, determining the individual rights of members of the community. Thus, should a judge appeal, say, to public safety, to justify some abstract right, this should be read as an appeal to the competing rights of those whose security will be forfeited if the abstract right is made concrete.

In a 'hard case'—like the homicidal beneficiary in *Riggs v. Palmer* (see earlier in the chapter)—no rule is immediately applicable. Thus the judge must apply standards other than rules. The ideal judge—whom Dworkin calls Hercules—must 'construct a scheme of abstract and concrete principles that provides a coherent justification for all common law precedents and, so far as these are to be justified on principle, constitutional and statutory principles as well'. Where the legal materials permit more than one consistent interpretation, Hercules will decide on the theory of law and justice which best coheres with the 'institutional history' of his community.

What if Hercules discovers a previous decision that does not 'fit' his own interpretation of the law? Suppose it is a precedent decided by a higher court which Hercules lacks the power to overrule? He may, says Dworkin, treat it as an 'embedded mistake', and confine it to having only 'enactment force'. This means its effect would be limited in future cases to its precise wording. Where, however, a previous judgment is neither overruled nor regarded as an embedded mistake, it will generate what Dworkin calls 'gravitational force', that is, it will exert an influence that extends beyond its actual wording: it will appeal to the fairness of treating like cases alike.

Dworkin contends that conventionalism (or legal positivism) is gravely impaired by arguments concerning the criteria of legal validity. As we saw in the last chapter, legal positivists are generally content with the fact that the rule of recognition stipulates that X is law. The pedigree of a rule is thus conclusive of its validity. But the basis of legal validity, Dworkin argues, cannot be determined solely by the standards contained in the rule of recognition. This constitutes what he calls the 'semantic sting' of legal positivism: positivist arguments about the law are really semantic disagreements concerning the meaning of the word 'law'.

But Dworkin argues that the concept of legal validity is more than mere promulgation in accordance with the rule of recognition. Semantic theories contest the claim that there are universal standards that exhaust the conditions for the proper application of the concept of law. Such theories, Dworkin argues, erroneously suppose that significant disagreement is impossible unless there are criteria for determining when our claims are sound, even if we cannot accurately specify what these criteria are.

Dworkin unscathed?

'Dworkin has in the course of five decades argued, over and again, that there are right answers to questions of value, and spelt out the implications of that fact for the social practice of law, for instance, in his famous theory of rights. Perhaps it is due to the bafflement, not to say offense, caused by this that he hasn't yet met his great critic. No one has yet effectively attacked his theories of law and politics on the grand scale as Hart did on Bentham, and Dworkin, himself, did on Hart. I believe Dworkin makes an excellent case . . . for saying that arguments about value are, relative to those in science, underdeveloped and misunderstood.'

Stephen Guest, *Ronald Dworkin*, 3, p. 1

Liberalism

His rights thesis is based on a form of liberalism that derives from the view that 'government must treat people as equals'. It may not impose any sacrifice or constraint on any citizen that the citizen could not accept without abandoning a sense of equal worth. His analysis of political morality has three ingredients: 'justice', 'fairness', and 'procedural due process'. 'Justice' incorporates both individual rights and collective goals which would be recognized by the ideal legislator dedicated to treating citizens with equal concern and respect. 'Fairness' refers to those procedures that give all citizens roughly equal influence in decisions that affect them. 'Procedural due process' relates to the correct procedures for determining whether a citizen has violated the law.

Upon this foundation of political liberalism, Dworkin has launched numerous forays against, for example, the enforcement by the criminal law of private morality, the idea of wealth as a value, and the alleged injustice of positive discrimination.

His purpose is to 'define and defend a liberal theory of law'. And this is the mainspring of his assault on positivism, conventionalism, and pragmatism. None of these theories of law provides an adequate defence of individual rights. It is only 'law as integrity' (see later) which affords a suitable defence against the advance by instrumentalism upon individual rights and general liberty.

Law as literature

A key component of Dworkinian legal theory is its claimed affinity to literary interpretation. When we attempt to interpret a work of art, Dworkin argues, we seek to understand it in a particular way. We try to portray the book, movie, poem, or picture accurately. We want to establish, as far as we are able, the intentions of the author in a *constructive* manner. Why did Henry James choose to write about these particular characters? What was his purpose? In answering these sorts of questions, we characteristically attempt to give the best account of the novel we can.

Law, claims Dworkin, like a novel or a play, requires interpretation. Judges are like interpreters of a developing story. They acknowledge their duty to preserve rather than reject their judicial tradition. They therefore develop, in response to their own beliefs and instincts, theories of the most constructive interpretation of their obligations within that tradition. We should therefore think of judges as authors engaged in a chain novel, each one of whom is required to write a new chapter which is added to what the next co-novelist receives. Each novelist attempts to make a single novel out of the previous chapters, endeavouring to write his or her chapter so that the ultimate result will be coherent. To accomplish this, he or she requires a vision of the story as it proceeds: its characters, plot, theme, genre, and general purpose. He or she will try to find the meaning in the evolving creation, and an interpretation that best justifies it.

Dworkin maintains that law is, like literature, an 'interpretive concept'. Judges 'normally recognise a duty to continue rather than discard the practice they have joined. So they develop, in response to their own convictions and instincts, working theories about *the best interpretation of their responsibilities under that practice*.' Thus, in the same way as you and I might disagree about the *real* meaning intended by a novelist in his or her work, two judges might disagree about the soundest interpretation of the relevant aspect of judicial practice. But note that Dworkin acknowledges that the author's intentions are merely one possible candidate for according the work its most constructive interpretation. Nor does he argue that constructive interpretation is always or essentially the interpretation of such intentions (rather than the interpretation of the work of art).

Dworkin seeks to apply this form of interpretation to a *social* practice. He asks us to imagine a community whose members follow a set of rules which they call 'rules of courtesy'. Various such rules exist requiring, for instance, that peasants doff their caps to nobility. Eventually members of the society begin to develop two approaches toward these rules: they assume that the rules have a certain *value* (i.e. they serve some purpose) independent of their mere existence, and they regard the requirements of courtesy as flexible—the strict rules need to be adapted or modified to meet changing needs. Once people have made these two assumptions, they have adopted an 'interpretive' view of courtesy: the institution of courtesy ceases to be mechanical. Members of the community now try to impose some *meaning* on it: to view courtesy in its best light, and then to reinterpret it in the light of that meaning. If a philosopher, call him Tom, wishes to explain this particular social practice, he would not be assisted by a theory which confined itself to a set of semantic rules which declare the proper use of the word 'courtesy'. He would fall prey to what Dworkin calls the 'semantic sting'. The only way Tom can explain this behaviour is by imposing a certain structure on the community's practices such that particular theories can be identified and understood as sub-interpretations of a more abstract idea. In other words, Tom's claim is 'interpretive' rather than semantic: it is not a claim about *linguistic* ground rules that everyone must follow to make sense.

This, argues Dworkin, is true of law. Semantic theories (such as those proffered by legal positivists) fail to explain the essence of law. Debates concerning whether evil 'laws' are indeed 'laws' are sterile if conducted at the *semantic* level: this merely relates to the meaning of 'law'—at what Dworkin calls the 'preinterpretive' stage. It becomes a more stimulating and significant debate at the *interpretive* level, for then the question becomes, not one of mere semantics, but one about the *substance* of law. For someone to claim that Nazi law is not 'law' then represents a sceptical interpretive judgment that Nazi law lacked those features vital to flourishing legal systems whose rules and procedures justify coercion. This is, in effect, a political judgment.

Law as integrity

As a constructive interpreter of the preceding chapters of the law, Hercules, the superhuman judge, will espouse the best account of the concept of law. And, in Dworkin's view, that consists in what he calls 'law as integrity'. This obliges Hercules to enquire whether his interpretation of the law could form part of a coherent theory justifying the whole legal system. What is 'integrity'? Dworkin offers the following description of its important elements:

> [L]aw as integrity accepts law and legal rights wholeheartedly... It supposes that law's constraints benefit society not just by providing predictability or procedural fairness, or in some other instrumental way, but *by securing a kind of equality among citizens that makes their community more genuine and improves its moral justification for exercising the political power it does*.... It argues that rights and responsibilities flow from past decisions and so count as legal, not just when they are explicit in these decisions but also when they follow from the principles of personal and political morality the explicit decisions presuppose by way of justification.

The collective application of coercion is defensible only when a society accepts integrity as a political virtue. This enables it to justify its moral authority to exercise a monopoly of force. Integrity is also a safeguard against partiality, deceit, and corruption. It ensures that the law is conceived as a matter of principle—addressing all members of the community as equals. It is, in short, an amalgam of values which form the essence of the liberal society and the rule of law, or, as Dworkin, has now called it, 'legality'.

Why do we value the law? Why do we respect those societies that adhere to the law and, more importantly, celebrate their observance of those political virtues that characterize states 'under law'? We do so, Dworkin suggests in his more recent work, because, while an efficient government is laudable, there is a greater value that is served by legality. A concern with the moral legitimacy of the law is a primary element of Dworkin's legal philosophy. It is based, in large part, on the rather imprecise concept of 'community' or 'fraternity'.

A political society that accepts integrity becomes a special form of community because it asserts its moral authority to use coercion. Integrity entails a kind of reciprocity between citizens, and an acknowledgement of the significance of their 'associative obligation'. A community's social practices spawn genuine obligations when it is a true, not merely a 'bare', community. This occurs when its members consider their obligations as special (i.e. applying specifically to the group), personal (i.e. flowing between members), and based on the equal concern for the welfare of all. Where these four conditions are satisfied, members of a bare community acquire the obligations of a true one.

Dworkin constructs his idea of political legitimacy upon this notion of a true community. Political obligation, he argues, is an illustration of associative obligation. To generate political obligations, a community must be a true community. It is only a community that supports the ideal of integrity that can be a genuine, morally legitimate, associative community—because its choices relate to obligation rather than naked force.

Comparing the judicial function to the process of literary criticism accentuates the positive portrayal of law and the fundamental role of judges within it. And Dworkin's conception of a political community as an association of principle is a powerfully attractive one. It is a condition which few societies will achieve, but to which, one hopes, many aspire.

Law and value

Dworkin's *Justice for Hedgehogs* takes its title from Isaiah Berlin's celebrated reference to Archilochus's aphorism comparing the fox and the hedgehog: 'The fox knows many things but the hedgehog knows one big thing'. That 'big thing' is what Dworkin calls the 'unity of value'. Endorsing what he calls 'Hume's principle' (that facts about the world or human nature cannot normally ordain what ought to be), he argues that Hume's distinction between fact and value, far from encouraging philosophical scepticism, actually weakens it because 'the proposition that it is not true that genocide is morally wrong *is itself a moral proposition*, and, if Hume's principle is sound, that proposition cannot be established by any discoveries of logic or facts about the basic structure of the universe. Hume's principle, properly understood, supports not scepticism about moral truth but rather the importance of morality as a separate department of knowledge with its own standards of inquiry and justification'.

This claim is fundamental to Dworkin's theory that moral values are both independent and objective. He insists upon the autonomy of arguments of value, rejecting the idea that external forces could induce a conflict between our values. Instead we should adhere to our value judgments, justifying them by reference to our more abstract values. We are responsible for making our moral views as clear and coherent as we can. And we are obliged to make our lives as good as we can:

> Someone lives well when he senses and pursues a good life for himself and does so with dignity: with respect for the importance of other people's lives and for their ethical responsibility as well as his own. The two ethical principles—living well and having a good life—are different. We can live well without having a good life: we may suffer bad luck or great poverty or serious injustice or a terrible disease or premature death. The value of our striving is adverbial; it does not lie in the goodness or impact of the life realized. That is

> why people who live and die in great poverty can nevertheless live well... You live badly if you do not try hard enough to make your life good.

We must live lives of 'dignity', this requires not only that we take our lives seriously, but that we also assume responsibility for our lives. Living a life of dignity promotes self-respect. This is a question of *ethics*. In addition, we owe *moral* duties towards others. For Dworkin, moral questions are an extension of ethics. By acknowledging the significance of self-respect, we are obliged—if we are to be logically consistent—to recognize its importance in the lives of others.

Almost every element of Dworkin's wide-ranging theories has provoked energetic, and occasionally even rancorous, debate. His ever-expanding group of detractors adopts a variety of standpoints from which to launch their assault upon what is a large, and sometimes moving, target. And there are no signs that the disagreement is likely to diminish.

Chapter 4
Rights and justice

Legal philosophy is inconceivable without an examination of the fundamental ideas of rights and justice. Rights, legal and moral, pervade the law and legal system, and are thus a central concern of jurisprudence. And the ideal of justice is both a vaunted virtue of domestic legal systems and, in its claims of universality, aspires to transcend law itself.

Individuals and groups are nowadays quick to assert their right to almost anything, and are no less adroit in claiming that their rights have been violated. Increasing pressure is put on governments and international organizations to safeguard and advance the rights of women, of minorities, and of citizens in general. The enactment of bills of rights in many countries has imposed new duties on courts to recognize rights that are either explicitly or implicitly protected.

What is a right? Is there a distinction between my rights as recognized by the law, and rights that I believe I ought to have? What of the problems generated by the escalating variety of human rights that individuals demand? Is it appropriate to insist on such rights when—in the case, say, of the right to work or the right to education—they entail considerable public expenditure?

While legal theory seeks answers to some of these questions, its chief preoccupation has been to define the concept of a right, and to develop theories to support or explain the nature of rights, and how competing rights are to be reconciled.

There are two major theories of rights. The first is known as the 'will' theory, and holds that, when I have a right to do something, what is effectively protected is my choice whether or not to do it. It accentuates my freedom and self-fulfilment. The second theory, known as the 'interest' theory, claims that the purpose of rights is to protect—not my individual choice, but certain of my interests. It is generally regarded as a superior account of what it is to have a right.

Those who espouse this theory raise two main arguments against the will theory. First, they refute the view that the essence of a right is the power to waive someone else's duty. Sometimes, they argue, the law limits my power of waiver without destroying my substantive right (e.g. I cannot consent to murder or contract out of certain rights). Second, there is a distinction between the substantive right and the right to enforce it. Thus children clearly lack the capacity or choice to waive such rights, but it would be absurd, they say, to argue that therefore children have no rights.

Hohfeld

The springboard for any analysis of rights is normally the well-known analysis by the American jurist, Wesley Hohfeld (1879–1918). He attempted to elucidate the proposition 'X has a right to do R' which he argued could mean one of four things. First, it could mean that Y (or anyone else) is under a duty to allow X to do R; this means, in effect, that X has a *claim* against Y. He calls this claim right simply a 'right'. Second, it might mean that X is free to do or refrain from doing something; Y owes *no duty* to X. He calls this a 'privilege' (though it is often described as a 'liberty'). Third, it could mean that X has a power to do R; X is simply free to do an act which alters legal rights and duties or legal relations in general (e.g. sell his property), whether or not he has a claim right or privilege to do so. Hohfeld calls this a 'power'.

Finally, it might suggest that X is not subject to Y's (or anyone's) power to change X's legal position. He calls this an 'immunity'.

Each of these four 'rights', Hohfeld argues, has both 'opposites' and 'correlatives' (i.e. the other side of the same coin) as shown in the box.

Hohfeld's scheme of 'jural relations'

Opposites	right	privilege	power	immunity
	no-right	duty	disability	liability
Correlatives	right	privilege	power	immunity
	duty	no-right	liability	disability

In other words, to use Hohfeld's own example, if X has a *right* against Y that Y shall stay off X's land, the *correlative* (and equivalent) is that Y is under a *duty* to keep off the land. A *privilege* is the *opposite* of a *duty*, and the *correlative* of a *no-right*. Hence, whereas X has a *right* (or *claim*) that Y should stay off his land, X himself has the *privilege* of entering on the land, or, in other words, X does not have a duty to stay off.

Claim rights (i.e. rights in the ordinary sense) are, Hohfeld maintains, strictly *correlative* to duties. To say that X has a claim right of some kind is to say that Y (or someone else) owes a certain duty to X. But to say that X has a certain liberty is *not* to say that anyone owes him a duty. Thus, if X has a *privilege* (or liberty) to wear a hat, Y does not have a *duty* to X, but a *no-right* that X should not wear a hat. In other words, the correlative of a liberty is a no-right. Similarly, the correlative of a power is a liability (i.e. being liable to have one's legal relations changed by another), the correlative of an immunity is a disability (i.e. the inability to change another's legal relations).

This analysis has been extremely influential, even though it suffers from certain limitations. All four of Hohfeld's rights (which, in modern accounts, are usually called claim rights, liberties, powers, and immunities) are rights *against a specific person or persons*. But it does not seem to be true that, whenever I am under some duty, someone else has a corresponding right. Or vice versa. Can I not have a duty without you (or anyone else) having a right that I should perform it? Thus, the criminal law imposes certain duties on me (say, to observe the rules of the road), but no specific person has a correlative right to my performing these duties. This is because it is possible for there to be a duty to do something which is not a duty owed to *someone*. For example, a police officer is under a clear duty to report offenders; but he or she owes this duty to no one in particular, and, hence, it gives rise to no right in anyone.

And even where someone owes a duty to *someone* to do something, the person to whom he or she owes such a duty does not necessarily have any corresponding right. Thus, a teacher has certain duties towards his or her students, but this does not necessarily confer any rights upon them. Similarly, we acknowledge our duties to infants or animals; yet many would claim that it does not follow from this that they have rights. On the other hand, an advantage of a theory of rights based on correlativity is that the claimant of a right to, say, employment, is compelled to identify the party who is under a corresponding duty to find him a job!

Rights theory

We live in the age of rights. Human rights, animal rights, moral and political rights play a leading role in public debate. But in addition to rights-based theories, some moral and legal philosophers adopt either duty-based or goal-based theories.

The differences between the three is worth noting, and may be illustrated as follows. You are opposed to torture because of the suffering of the victim (this is rights-based), or because torture debases the torturer (duty-based), or you may regard torture as unacceptable only when it affects the interests of those other than the parties involved (utilitarian goal-based).

Ronald Dworkin's theory of law is underpinned by his rights thesis (see Chapter 3). Rights are trumps. The right to equal concern and respect is fundamental to human dignity and to a fair society. Equality is assigned primacy over liberty. And the ideal of equal rights has had a spectacular impact in numerous societies; think of the Civil Rights movement in the 1950s in the United States, and the collapse of apartheid in South Africa (Figure 7).

7. Nelson Mandela with the author soon after the former South African president's release from 27 years of imprisonment. A trained lawyer, Mandela's dedication to the overthrow of apartheid made him an international symbol of the struggle against injustice, and a champion of the establishment of liberty and equality under law

Constitutional change has been wrought through the strength of legal and moral argument based on the relatively uncomplicated concept of human equality.

The concept of human rights has acquired a prominent place in contemporary political and legal debate today. Turn on the news or read a newspaper: issues of human rights are ubiquitous. Though the concept (in the form of 'natural rights' see Chapter 1) first emerges in the Middle Ages, the recognition in the 17th and 18th centuries of the secular notion of human rights was a significant intellectual moment in history. The idea rests on the claim that each of us as a human being, regardless of our race, religion, gender, or age, is entitled to certain fundamental and inalienable rights—merely by virtue of our belonging to the human race. Whether or not such rights are legally recognized is irrelevant, as is the fact that they may or may not emanate from a 'higher' natural law (see Chapter 1).

The acceptance by the United Nations, in the aftermath of the Holocaust, of the Universal Declaration of Human Rights in 1948, and the International Covenants on Civil and Political Rights, and Economic, Social and Cultural Rights in 1976, reveals a dedication by the community of nations to the universal conception and protection of human rights (see Figure 8).

Human rights have passed through three generations. The first generation were mostly the negative civil and political rights as developed in the 17th and 18th centuries by English political philosophers like Hobbes, Locke, and Mill (see Chapter 1). They are negative in the sense that they generally prohibit interference with the right-holder's freedom. A good example is the First Amendment to the American Constitution, which makes it unlawful for the legislature to restrict a person's freedom of speech.

The second generation consists in the essentially positive economic, social, and cultural rights, such as the right to education, food, or medical care. The third generation of human

8. In the United States the campaign for equality before the law was protracted and painful. Racial prejudice assumed many forms, but the American South produced its own violent brand: between 1889 and 1918, 2,522 blacks were lynched, including 50 women

rights is primarily collective rights which are foreshadowed in Article 28 of the Universal Declaration. This declares that 'everyone is entitled to a social and international order in which the rights set forth in this Declaration can be fully realized'. These 'solidarity' rights include the right to social and economic development and to participate in and benefit from the resources of the earth and space, scientific and technical information (which are especially important to the Third World), the right to a healthy environment, peace, and humanitarian disaster relief.

Not every political right is human right. Yet human rights appear to be sufficiently important to justify international intervention when they are violated. The question, however, arises as to whether the breach of *any* human right validates the imposition by the United Nations of sanctions or even military intervention by NATO or other states, as has become increasingly common.

Would the infringement of *economic and social rights* permit such a breach of national sovereignty? The answer must be in the negative. As Dworkin has written:

> It would be…wrong for the community of nations, even if licensed by the Security Council and likely to be successful, to march into any nation to establish equal pay for women or more adequate schools or to invade Florida to shut down its gas chambers or establish gay marriages there. Economic or military sanctions that inevitably inflict great suffering…are justified only to stop truly barbaric acts: mass killing or jailing or torturing of political opponents or widespread and savage discrimination.

This suggests the recognition that certain human rights are more fundamental, more essential, and more universal, than others. If this is true, these 'positive', socio-economic rights, though frequently included in human rights declarations and bills of rights, are of a different order from 'negative' political rights. This dichotomy has long bedevilled the argument, especially since, even if socio-economic rights were justiciable (which may be doubted) it is questionable whether unelected judges should have the power to determine how the economic resources should be distributed.

Indeed, despite its appeal and importancc, the idea of human rights remains exasperatingly vague, if not incoherent. It is difficult to disagree with James Griffin's sober assessment:

> The term 'human right' is nearly criterionless. There are unusually few criteria for determining when the term is used correctly and when incorrectly—not just among politicians, but among philosophers, political theorists, and jurisprudents as well. The language of human rights has, in this way, become debased.

But are human rights really universal? To what extent are they 'relative' to local culture, history, and social and political conditions? Cultural relativists, for example, claim that human rights declarations overlook parochial diversity, and although this approach has a fairly long pedigree in anthropology, it has only fairly recently entered human rights discourse. The doctrine maintains that in the words of the philosopher, John Ladd, 'there is an irreducible diversity among cultures because each culture is a unique whole with parts so intertwined that none of them can be understood or evaluated without reference to the other parts and so to the cultural whole, the so-called pattern of culture'.

Two main arguments may be deployed against the relativist. The first denies that morality depends on social factors at all; this may therefore be described as the *absolutist* position. The second denies the assertion that there has always been a diversity of cultures, and so on, and a diversity of moral beliefs. This is known as *universalism*.

The absolutist position was held by Plato and claims that the validity of moral beliefs is logically independent of the social or cultural background of the person who accepts them; ethics is no less a scientific enterprise than mathematics. This position is vulnerable to the charge that it divorces moral thinking from the 'real world'; it compels us to think about morality in a vacuum.

The universalist view is often stigmatized as ethnocentric for its failure to appreciate cultural practices from the perspective of the culture in which a particular practice is transacted.

Justice

The law is frequently equated with justice. Courts are designated 'courts of justice', their buildings flamboyantly emblazoned with the word itself, or its symbolic representations of equity and fairness. Governments create ministries of 'justice' to oversee the administration of the legal system. Alleged offenders are no longer charged or prosecuted, but 'brought to justice'. But caution is required. The law occasionally deviates from justice. Worse, it may actually be an instrument of injustice, as in Nazi Germany or apartheid South Africa. Though the law may, in virtuous societies, aspire to justice, it is mistaken to bracket the two together.

Justice, in any event, is a far from simple concept. Most discussions of the subject begin with Aristotle's claim that justice consists in treating equals equally and 'unequals' unequally, in proportion to their inequality. He distinguished between 'corrective' justice (where a court redresses a wrong committed by one party against another), and 'distributive' justice (which seeks to give each person his or her due according to what is deserved). Distributive justice in Aristotle's view was chiefly the concern of the legislator. But he does not tell us what justice actually is.

We gain somewhat clearer guidance from the Romans. The *Corpus Juris Civilis* is the body of civil law codified under the order of the Emperor Justinian (*c*.482–565). Justice is there defined as 'the constant and perpetual wish to give everyone that which they deserve'. And the 'precepts of the law' are stated to be 'to live honestly, not to injure others, and to give everyone his due'. These expressions, though fairly general, do contain at least three important overlapping features of any conception of justice. It conveys the importance of the individual; second, that individuals be treated consistently and impartially; and, third, that they be treated equally.

The significance of impartiality as a key element of justice is often depicted in material form as Themis, the goddess of justice and law. She typically clutches a sword in one hand and a pair of scales in the other. The sword signifies the power of those who occupy judicial positions; the scales symbolize the neutrality and impartiality with which justice is served. In the 16th century, artists portrayed her blindfolded to emphasize justice is blind: resistant to pressure or influence (Figure 9).

9. The so-called goddess of justice wears a blindfold, and clutches a pair of scales in one hand, and a sword in the other. This statue stands above the Central Criminal Court (the 'Old Bailey') in London

Equality seems helpful in our search for a satisfactory concept of justice. Treating equals equally and unequals unequally has a certain appeal—provided we can agree on objectively ascertainable and relevant grounds for distinguishing between individuals. One criterion might be their different needs. Elizabeth is rich, James is poor. Would a reasonable person object to providing resources to him rather than to her? One might if the cause of James' poverty is his profligacy and extravagance. The principle of need is therefore not without difficulty.

What of desert? Can justice be made to turn on what individuals deserve? It is often said that someone got his or her 'just deserts', suggesting that since Doris worked hard, she deserves her promotion over Boris. But Boris may lack Doris's drive because he has to support several dependants and fatigue is an impediment to his commitment to his job. Since he lacks complete control over his depressing domestic predicament, basing justice on desert could actually generate injustice!

Justice between individuals is no less problematic than the challenge of social justice: the establishment of social and political institutions to slice the cake fairly. Modern accounts of justice are inclined to focus on how society can most fairly distribute the burdens and benefits of social life. One especially influential theory is that of utilitarianism, and its modern alternative, the economic analysis of law. The rest of this chapter is devoted to considering this approach to justice. I shall then sketch the main features of John Rawls's celebrated theory of 'justice as fairness'.

Utilitarianism

Justice, according to utilitarians, lies in the maximization of happiness. Most famously, Jeremy Bentham (whose positivist theories we examined in Chapter 2) argued that, since in our daily lives, we strive to be happy and avoid pain, so too should society be structured to realize this objective:

> Nature has placed humankind under the governance of two sovereign masters, *pain* and *pleasure*. It is for them alone to point out what we ought to do, as well as to determine what we shall do. On the one hand the standard of right and wrong, on the other the chain of causes and effects, are fastened to their throne.... The *principle of utility* recognizes this subjection, and assumes it for the foundation of that system, the object of which is to rear the fabric of felicity by the hands of reason and of law. Systems which attempt to question it, deal in sounds instead of sense, in caprice instead of reason, in darkness instead of light.

The determining factor is thus the outcome of our actions: do they make us happy or sad? Through the application of a 'felicific calculus', he argued, we can test the 'happiness factor' of any action or rule. Utilitarianism thus looks to the consequences of actions; it is therefore described as a form of 'consequentialism' which must be distinguished from deontological systems of ethics which hold that the rightness or wrongness of an action is logically independent of its consequences—'Let justice be done though the heavens fall!' is one of its uplifting slogans.

It is important to note that utilitarians distinguish between 'act utilitarianism' (the rightness or wrongness of an action is to be judged by the consequences, good or bad, of the action itself) and 'rule utilitarianism' (the rightness or wrongness of an action is to be judged by the goodness or badness of the consequences of a rule that everyone should perform the action in like circumstances).

Generally, discussions of utilitarianism concern themselves with 'act utilitarianism', though legal theorists often appeal to 'ideal rule utilitarianism' which provides that the rightness or wrongness of an action is to be judged by the goodness or badness of a rule which, *if observed*, would have better consequences than any other rule governing the same action. This form of rule utilitarianism has clear advantages in circumstances where a judge is called upon to decide whether the plaintiff should be awarded damages against the defendant. He or she must obviously disregard the result of his or her judgment on the particular defendant.

Modern utilitarians tend to regard Bentham's version of hedonistic act utilitarianism as rather quaint. Nor is there a great deal of contemporary sympathy for John Stuart Mill's form of utilitarianism that distinguishes between higher and lower pleasures—implying that pleasure is a necessary condition for goodness, but that goodness depends on qualities of experience other than pleasantness and unpleasantness. This may be because both Bentham and Mill appear to substitute their own preferences for the preferences they believe people *ought* to have.

Contemporary utilitarians therefore talk of maximizing the extent to which people may achieve what they *want*; we should seek to satisfy people's *preferences*. This has the merit of not imposing any conception of 'the good' which leaves out of account individual choice: you may prefer football to Foucault, or Motown to Mozart. But this approach is afflicted with its own problems; see later.

Evaluating the consequences of our actions

I am stranded on a desert island with no one but a dying man who, in his final hours, entrusts me with $10,000 which he asks me to give to his daughter, Rita, if I ever manage to return to the United States. I promise to do so, and, after my rescue, I find Rita living in a mansion; she has married a millionaire. The $10,000 will now make little difference to her financial situation. Should I not instead donate the money to charity? As a utilitarian, I consider the possible consequences of my action. But what are the consequences? I must weigh the result of my broken promise against the benefit of giving the $10,000 to an animal welfare charity. Would keeping my promise have better consequences than breaking it? If I break my promise, I may be less likely to keep other promises I have made, and others may be encouraged to take their own promise-keeping less seriously. I must, in other words, attempt to calculate all the likely consequences of my choice. But a non-consequentialist Kantian might argue that the reason why I should give the money to Rita is that I have promised to do so. My action ought to be guided not by some uncertain future consequence, but by an unequivocal past fact: my promise. My reply might be that I do consider the past fact of my promise—but only to the extent that it affects the total consequences of my action of giving the money to the charity instead of to Rita.
I might also say that it is absurd to argue that I am obliged to keep every promise I make.

Utilitarianism has the considerable attraction of replacing moral intuition with the congenially down-to-earth idea of human happiness as a measure of justice. But the theory has long encountered resistance from those who argue that it fails to recognize the 'separateness of persons'. They claim that utilitarianism, at least in its pure form, regards human beings as means rather than ends in themselves. Separate individuals, it is contended, are important to utilitarians only in so far as they are 'the channels or locations where what is of value is to be found'.

Second, opponents of utilitarianism claim that, though the approach treats individual persons equally, it does so only by effectively regarding them as having no worth: their value is not as persons, but as 'experiencers' of pleasure or happiness. Third, critics query why we should regard as a valuable moral goal the mere increase in the sum of pleasure or happiness abstracted from all questions of the *distribution* of happiness, welfare, and so on.

A fourth kind of attack alleges that the analogy, used by utilitarians, of a rational single individual prudently sacrificing present happiness for later satisfaction, is false for it treats my pleasure as replaceable by the greater pleasure of others. Some have attacked the assumption at the very heart of utilitarianism: why should we seek to satisfy people's desires? Certain desires—e.g. cruelty to animals—are unworthy of satisfaction. And are our needs and desires not, in any event, subject to manipulation by advertising? If so, can we detach our 'real' preferences from our 'conditioned' ones? Is it then acceptable for utilitarians to seek to persuade individuals to prefer Dworkin to Doo Wop? If so, how do we justify doing this? If we answer that the principle of utility requires us to do it, are we not suggesting that the felicific calculus includes not only what we want, but also what we may one day decide we want as a result of persuasion or re-education?

A different point is made by John Rawls who argues that utilitarianism defines what is right in terms of what is 'good'. This means that the theory starts with a conception of what is 'good' (e.g. happiness) and then concludes that an action is *right* in so far as it maximizes that 'good'.

Should we, in any event, seek to maximize welfare? Some consider it more important that welfare be justly distributed. Another target of critics is the intractable problem of calculating the consequences of one's actions: how can we know in advance what results will follow from what we propose to do. And how far into the future do—or can—we extend the consequences of our actions?

There are obvious difficulties in attempting to weigh my pleasure against your pain. Similarly, on a larger scale, judges or legislators will rarely find it easy to choose between two or more courses of action, and sensibly balance the majority's happiness against a minority's misery.

The economic analysis of law

Like utilitarianism, those who champion an economic analysis of law believe that our rational everyday choices ought to form the basis of what is just in society.

This modern form of utilitarianism has, as its launching-pad, the idea that the rational man or woman always chooses to do that which will maximize his or her satisfactions. And this latter-day pragmatic economic hedonism claims that if they want something badly enough they will be prepared to *pay* for it. The *raison d'être* of the theory is the notion of wealth-maximization which, its supporters claim, provides the benefits of utilitarianism without its drawbacks. It would, moreover, be chosen as the most attractive option by most people.

Its leading light, judge and jurist Richard Posner (b. 1939) denies that he adopts a utilitarian position. He contends that a good deal of the common law can be explained by this simple fact of life. Moreover, Posner argues, courts frequently decide difficult cases by choosing an outcome which maximizes the wealth of society. By 'wealth maximization' Posner means a situation in which goods and other resources are in the hands of those people who *value them most*; that is to say, those people who are willing (and able) to *pay* more to have them.

So, for example, if I buy your copy of *The Economic Analysis of Law* for $10 when the most I was *willing* to pay for it was $12, my wealth has been increased by $2. Similarly, society maximizes its wealth when all its resources are distributed in such a way that the sum of everyone's transactions is as high as possible. And this, according to Posner, is as it *should* be; his theory is therefore both descriptive and normative. Moreover, in a series of essays, he and other members of the so-called Chicago School that emerged in the 1960s, attempt to show how common law judges have (generally unconsciously) been guided by these economic considerations.

Posner repudiates the autonomy of law on two grounds. First, he denies that law develops independently of social and economic forces. Second, he asserts that non-legal disciplines—particularly economics—have an indispensable role to play in our understanding of the law. His argument in support of the importance of economic factors is thus, as just mentioned, both descriptive (economics actually determines judicial outcomes) and normative (the efficient allocation of resources ought to guide judges in their judgments). The economic analysis inevitably deploys a number of technical concepts such as 'optimality', 'transaction costs', 'damage costs', 'precaution costs', and so on. Some are less daunting than others.

Very briefly, the test of Pareto optimality (named after the Italian economist Vilfredo Pareto) describes a situation which cannot be altered without making at least one person think he or she is worse off than prior to the change. In other words, the profit of one party can be increased only by reducing the profit of another party. And the Kaldor–Hicks test is satisfied when the alteration in the allocation of resources produces enough money to compensate those who are losers. The concept of 'diminishing marginal utility' refers to the fact that £5 given to an impoverished beggar would have a major effect on his wealth, whereas to a millionaire, £5 would make no difference at all.

The renowned Coase theorem (after the British Nobel laureate, Ronald Coase, 1910–2013) postulates a situation in which one outcome is the most 'efficient'. Real life is, however, more complex: some costs would be incurred in this process. The simple version of the Coase theorem may be stated as follows: where there are zero transaction costs, the efficient outcome will occur regardless of the choice of legal rule. The theorem has assumed great importance in economic theory, especially for 'economists of law' who have applied it in the quest for just solutions—at least where one is able to place an economic value on costs and benefits, for example when measuring the efficiency of systems of accident compensation.

The approach of the law and economics movement is far from uncontroversial. Have economic factors really played such a significant role in decisions by judges? Is wealth maximization truly a 'value' (in itself or instrumentally) that a society would regard as worth trading off against justice? Does the analysis oversimplify individual choice? Does the approach not merely reflect a particular ideological preference: the capitalist, free-market system? What does it have to do with *justice*? It presupposes an *initial* distribution of wealth—which may be wholly unjust. 'Efficiency' therefore becomes a means of rationalizing, and sustaining, existing inequalities. And can we—should we—reduce life to the single measure of wealth?

Economic analysis is now used fairly widely by policy-makers and even courts, especially in the United States. It is more congenial to the former, where legislators attempt to predict the outcome of competing policies and thereby better to reform the law. In respect of the adjudicative process, however, one may query whether many judges have the requisite training and skill to determine the validity or otherwise of the arguments presented to them. Even Judge Posner would surely concede that not all judges are Richard Posner.

Justice as fairness

A Theory of Justice by John Rawls (1921–2002) is widely regarded as a *tour de force*. It expounds the concept of justice as fairness, and has—justly—become the focal point for contemporary discussions of the subject.

The idea of justice as fairness may, at first blush, strike you as trite. But, in dismissing utilitarianism as a means of determining justice, Rawls rejects the very idea of inequality—even if it secures maximum welfare. Welfare, he argues, is not about benefits, but 'primary social goods' which includes self-respect. In particular, he contends that questions of justice are prior to questions of happiness. In other words, it is only when we regard a particular pleasure as just that we can judge whether it has any value. How can we know whether the gratification Tom derives from torture should be counted as having any value before we know whether the practice of torture is itself just? Put another way, utilitarianism defines what is right in terms of what is good, while Rawls considers what is right as prior to what is good (see Figure 10).

Chapter 1 touched on the social contract theories of Hobbes, Locke, and Rousseau. Rawls's theory of justice as fairness is rooted in this enduring idea. In *A Theory of Justice*, he expresses the objective of his project as carrying the social contract to a higher level of abstraction. To do so, he argues, we are to think not that

10. John Rawls's theory of justice as fairness has exerted considerable influence on the analysis of this difficult concept

the original contract as one to enter a particular society or to set up a particular form of government, but that the principles of justice for the basic structure of society are the object of the original agreement. They are the principles that free and rational persons seeking to further their own interests would accept in an initial position of equality as defining the fundamental terms of their association. These principles regulate all further agreements; they specify the types of social cooperation and the forms of government that can be established. This manner of treating the principles of justice he calls justice as fairness.

He stresses the need to distinguish between people's genuine judgements about justice and their subjective, self-interested intuitions. The inevitable distinction between the two must be adjusted by re-examining our own judgements so that we ultimately reach a state of affairs in which our considered intuitions are in harmony with our considered principles. This is the position of 'reflective equilibrium'.

Rawls presents an imaginary picture of the people in the 'original position', shrouded in a 'veil of ignorance', debating the principles of justice. They do not know their gender, class, religion, or social position. Each person represents a social class, but they do not know whether they are intelligent or dim, strong or weak, or even the country or period in which they are living. And they have only certain elementary knowledge about the laws of science and psychology.

In this state of almost perfect ignorance, they are required unanimously to choose the general principles that will define the terms under which they will live as a society. In this process they are motivated by rational self-interest: each seeks those principles which will give him or her (but they are unaware of their gender!) the greatest opportunity of accomplishing his or her chosen conception of the good life. Stripped of their individuality, the people in the original position will select, says Rawls, a 'maximin' principle which is explained by Rawls's own gain and loss table (slightly adapted).

I am faced with a choice from a number of several possible circumstances. Suppose I choose D1, and C1 occurs. I will lose $700. But if C2 occurs, I will gain $800 and, if I am really fortunate and C3 occurs, I will gain $1,200. And the same applies in the case of both decisions D2 and D3. Gain *g* therefore depends on the individual's decision *d* and the circumstances *c*. Thus *g* is a function of *d* and *c*. Or, to express it mathematically $g = f(d, c)$.

What would I choose? The 'maximin' principle dictates that I opt for D3. In this situation the worst that can happen to me is that I gain $500, and this is clearly better than the worst for the other actions (in which I stand to lose either $800 or $700).

Decisions	**Circumstances**		
	C1	C2	C3
D1	–$700	$800	$1,200
D2	–$800	$700	$1,400
D3	$500	$600	$800

Exercising their choice, the people in the original position, as rational individuals, would also select principles that ensure that the worst condition one might find oneself in, when the veil of ignorance is lifted, is the least undesirable of the available alternatives. In other words, I will select those principles which, if I happen to end up at the bottom of the social order, will be in my best interests. Similarly, Rawls argues, the people in the original position will choose the following two principles:

1. Each person is to have an equal right to the most extensive total system of equal basic liberties compatible with a similar system of liberty for all.
2. Social and economic inequalities are to be arranged so that they are both:
   (a) to the greatest benefit of the least advantaged, consistent with the just savings principle, and
   (b) attached to offices and positions open to all under conditions of fair equality of opportunity.

The first principle has what Rawls calls 'lexical priority' over the second. In other words, the people in the original position place liberty before equality. Why? Because of the 'maximin' strategy, described above, no one wants to risk his or her liberty when the veil of ignorance is lifted—and it is revealed that they are among the least well-off members of society!

Similarly, each will opt for clause (a) of the second principle, the so-called 'difference principle'. This ensures that the worst anyone could be is 'least advantaged' and, if they do end up as members of this group, they will benefit from this clause. It would be entirely rational to choose this principle—rather than either total equality or some form of greater inequality—because of the respective risks of being worse off or reducing the prospects of improving their lot. And, in a society that puts liberty above equality, they will be in a better position to improve their lot. Why? Because various 'social primary goods' (which Rawls defines to include rights, liberties, powers, opportunities, income, wealth, and especially self-respect) are more likely to be attained in a society that protects liberty.

Rawls argues that the people in the original position will select the difference principle because neither of its two principal competitors (the 'system of natural liberty' and the idea of 'fair equality of opportunity') offers them the prospect of prosperity should they turn out to be among the least advantaged. The former corresponds to an uncontrolled, free-market economy indifferent to wealth distribution. The people in the original position would jettison this principle, he claims, because it 'permits distributive shares to be improperly influenced by... factors so arbitrary from a moral point of view'. They would regard the accident of being born into an affluent family as morally irrelevant.

They would spurn the second arrangement even though it is plainly preferable to the first. While it rewards natural talent and its application, this system suffers from a similar deficiency:

it attaches moral relevance to individual talent, but this is no less accidental than being the offspring of a millionaire. In neither situation, do accidents of birth have any association with desert. If they choose the difference principle, however, it guarantees that talented individuals may increase their wealth only if, in the process, they also increase the wealth of the least advantaged.

Note that Rawls's second principle includes two significant limitations to secure the interests of the least advantaged. First, he introduces the 'just savings principle' which requires the people in the original position to ask themselves how much they would be willing to save at each level of the advance of their society, on the assumption that all other generations will save at the same rate. Remember that they have no idea which stage of civilization their society has reached. Consequently they will save some of their resources for future generations. The second limitation refers to the fact that jobs should be available to all.

Rawls's project is a highly ambitious one and, while it has won enormous praise and generated a huge literature, critics have, not surprisingly, expressed reservations about several features of his theory. For example, some oppose the very idea of any patterned distribution of social goods. Others attack the 'original position' as artificial (can people really be wholly stripped of their values?) or as necessarily producing the result that Rawls postulates: why should they prefer liberty to equality?

In response to some of this criticism, Rawls published in 1993 another book, *Political Liberalism*, in which he refines and modifies a number of his original ideas. I cannot here analyse the plethora of critical debate, but an important misunderstanding is clarified in this later work. Rawls explains that 'justice as fairness' is not intended to provide a universal standard of social justice. His theory is a practical one that pertains to modern constitutional democracies. His is, in other words, a political and practical—rather than a metaphysical—conception of justice, philosophically neutral, that transcends philosophical argument.

In pursuit of what he calls an 'overlapping consensus', Rawls posits his principles of justice as the terms under which members of a pluralistic, democratic community with competing interests and values might achieve political accord. His conception of political liberalism acknowledges that this consensus may be challenged by a state's establishment of a shared moral or religious doctrine. But the community's sense of justice would prevail over the state's interpretation of the public good.

Chapter 5
Law and society

So far we have been preoccupied with normative legal theory, and its endeavours to explain the concept of law, as it were, from within. That is to say, normative legal theory concentrates on legal doctrine and the relations between rules, concepts, principles, and other constructs employed by courts and lawyers engaged in the actual practice of the law. But there is another approach to legal analysis that attempts to understand the nature of these phenomena by reference to the social conditions in which they function. This sociological approach has exerted a considerable influence, often unacknowledged, on the philosophy of law.

For example, Hart's insistence that officials accept the rule of recognition 'from the internal point of view' and his claim that there should be a 'critical reflective attitude' to certain patterns of behaviour as a common standard (see Chapter 2) echo Max Weber's concept of internal legitimation (see below).

A sociological account of law normally rests on three closely related claims: that law cannot be understood except as a 'social phenomenon', that an analysis of legal concepts provides only a partial explanation of 'law in action', and that law is merely one form of social control.

Though the genesis of sociological jurisprudence or the sociology of law may be traced back to the trail-blazing writings of Roscoe

Pound and Eugen Ehrlich, this chapter focuses on the two giants of social theory—Émile Durkheim and Max Weber—whose impact on jurisprudence has been most profound. I shall also have something to say about the impact of Karl Marx on thinking about law and the legal system, as well as about two leading social theorists, Jürgen Habermas and Michel Foucault, whose writings continue to exert a considerable influence in certain quarters of contemporary legal theory.

Émile Durkheim

Among the central preoccupations of Durkheim (1859–1917) is the question of what holds societies together. Why do they not drift apart? His answer points to the crucial role of law in promoting and maintaining this social cohesion. He shows how, as society advances from religion to secularism, and from collectivism to individualism, law becomes concerned less with punishment than with compensation. But punishment performs a significant role in expressing the collective moral attitudes by which social solidarity is preserved.

He distinguishes between what he calls mechanical solidarity and organic solidarity. The former exists in simple, homogeneous societies which have a uniformity of values and lack any significant division of labour. These uncomplicated communities tend to be collective in nature; there is very little individualism. In advanced societies, however, where there is division of labour, a high degree of interdependence exists. There is substantial differentiation, and collectivism is replaced by individualism. These forms of social solidarity are, he argues, reflected in the law: classify the different types of law and you will find the different types of social solidarity to which it corresponds.

Crime, according to Durkheim, is a perfectly normal aspect of social life. Moreover, he provocatively suggests, it is an integral part of all healthy societies. This is because crime is closely connected to the social values expressed in the 'collective conscience': an act becomes criminal when it offends deeply held aspects of this collective conscience. An action does not shock the common conscience because it is criminal, rather it is criminal because it shocks the common conscience.

Punishment is an essential element of his conception of crime: the state reinforces the collective conscience by punishing those who offend against the state itself. He defines punishment as 'a passionate reaction of graduated intensity that society exercises through the medium of a body acting upon those of its members who have violated certain rules of conduct'.

He shows also how punishment as a form of social control is more intense in less developed societies. As societies progress, the form of punishment becomes less violent and less harsh (Figure 11).

11. Primitive societies practised cruel punishments like burning at the stake. As societies progress, Durkheim argued, the form of punishment diminishes in its cruelty

But because punishment results from crime, he identifies an important correlation between the evolution of crime and the forms of social solidarity.

Max Weber

The German sociologist Max Weber (1864–1920) trained as lawyer, and he assigns to the law a central role in his general sociological theory. Weber's classification of the types of law is founded on the different kinds of legal thought, and 'rationality' is the key. On this basis, he distinguishes between 'formal' systems and 'substantive' systems. The crux of this distinction is the extent to which the system is 'internally self-sufficient', by which he means that the rules and procedures required for decision-making are accessible *within* the system.

His second critical distinction is between 'rational' and 'irrational': these terms describe the manner in which the materials (rules, procedures) are applied in the system. Thus the highest stage of rationality is reached where there is an

> integration of all analytically derived legal propositions in such a way that they constitute a logically clear, internally consistent, and, at least in theory, gapless system of rules, under which, it is implied, all conceivable fact situations must be capable of being logically subsumed.

Two principal, and related, elements of Weber's complex theory will be considered briefly here: his concern to explain the development of capitalism in Western societies and his notion of legitimate domination.

In respect of the first problem, he attempts to show that law is affected only indirectly by economic circumstances. He conceives of law as being 'relatively autonomous', claiming that 'generally it appears...that the development of the legal structure has by no means been predominantly determined by economic factors'. For Weber, law is *fundamentally related to*, but not *determined by*, economic factors. Rational economic conduct ('profit-making activity' and 'budgetary management') is at the heart of the capitalist system; this rationalism is facilitated by the certainty and predictability of logically formal rational law. The presence of this type of law assists, but does not cause, the advance of capitalism.

Weber regards formally rational law as one of the preconditions of capitalism because it provides the necessary certainty and predictability that is essential if entrepreneurs are to pursue their profit-making enterprises. The achievement of this formal rationality required, in Weber's view, the systematization of the legal order, a systematization which he found remarkably absent from the English law.

How, then, could he explain the emergence of capitalism in England? This question has troubled many sociologists. Three possible explanations are offered for this apparent contradiction in Weber's work. First, it is clear that, although English law lacked the systematic order of the Roman law, it was a highly formalistic legal system. Indeed, Weber characterized such formalism (which required, for example, civil actions to follow the precise and exacting procedures of specific writs for specific civil suits) as irrational. It was this very formalism, Weber says, that produced a stabilizing influence on the legal system; and it created a greater degree of security and predictability in the economic market-place.

Second, the English legal profession was, during the rise of capitalism, extremely centralized in London, close to the commercial district known as the City. Moreover, lawyers customarily served as advisers to businessmen and corporations. This encouraged them to adjust the law to suit the interests of their commercial clients.

Third, unlike their Continental counterparts, English lawyers resembled craft guilds in their education, training, and specialization, which produced a formalistic treatment of the law, bound by precedent. This led to what Weber calls, following Roman law, 'cautelary jurisprudence': emphasis is laid on drafting instruments and devising new clauses to prevent future litigation. This resulted in a close relationship between lawyers and their (mostly commercial) clients. In other words, this feature of legal practice compensated for the lack of systematization in the law itself.

It seems therefore that what Weber is really saying is that England developed a capitalist economic system, despite the absence of legal systematization, because other important components of the legal system engendered it, but that it may have developed even more rapidly and more efficiently if the common law had been less irrational and unsystematic.

Weber's general thesis is that the formal rationalization of law in Western societies is a result of capitalism interested in strictly formal law and legal procedure and 'the rationalism of officialdom in absolutist States [which] led to the interest in codified systems and in homogeneous law'. He is not seeking to provide an economic explanation for this phenomenon, but identifies several factors that account for the development, including, in particular, the growth of bureaucracy which established, as we saw above, the basis for the administration of a rational law conceptually systematized.

In explaining why people believe they are obliged to obey the law, Weber draws his famous distinction between three types of legitimate domination: *traditional* (where 'legitimacy is claimed for it and believed in by sanctity of age-old rules and powers'), *charismatic* (based on 'devotion to the exceptional sanctity, heroism or exemplary character of an individual person'), and *legal-rational* domination (which rests on 'a belief in the legality of enacted rules and the right of those elevated to authority under such rules to issue commands'). It is, of course, this third type that is a central feature of Weber's account of law. And, though the concept of legal-rational authority is bound up with his theory of value (which argues for the sociologist of law adopting a detached view of his subject), the important link is between this form of domination and the modern bureaucratic state.

Under the other forms of domination, authority resides in *persons*; under bureaucracy, it is vested in *rules*. The hallmark of legal-rational authority is its so-called impartiality. But it depends upon what Weber calls the principle of 'formalistic impersonality': officials exercise their responsibilities 'without hatred or passion, and hence without affection or enthusiasm. The dominant norms are concepts of straightforward duty without regard to personal considerations.' The importance of Weber's sociology of law lies in the correlation between the various typologies. For example, in a society with legal-rational domination, the form of legal thought is logical formal rationality: justice and the judicial process are both rational, obedience is owed to the legal order, and the form of administration is bureaucratic-professional.

On the other hand, in a society dominated by a charismatic leader, legal thought is formally and substantively irrational, justice is charismatic, obedience is in response to the charismatic leader, and in a society that is genuinely dominated by a charismatic leader, there is no administration at all.

While Weber is widely regarded as the leading sociologist of law, his detractors have found numerous flaws in his analysis, particularly in respect of the two theories I have sketched above. It is claimed, for example, that his account of the process of domination is more complex than the formal, legal manifestation upon which Weber focuses. And some find his attempt to explain the rise of capitalism in England unconvincing.

Karl Marx

While Karl Marx (1818–83) and Friedrich Engels (1820–95) do not provide a comprehensive or systematic account of law, their social theory bristles with observations about the relationship between law and economics (or material conditions). But the law is accorded an inferior position to economic factors: it is merely part of the superstructure—along with various cultural and political phenomena—determined by the material conditions of each society.

Marxist accounts of law adopt one of two standpoints in respect of the relationship between base and superstructure and the position of law. The first has been dubbed 'crude materialism' for it argues that the law simply 'reflects' the economic base: the form and content of legal rules correspond to the dominant mode of production. This is generally regarded as providing a simplistic and incoherent explanation of how the law does so. The second view is known as 'class instrumentalism' because it contends that the law is a direct expression of the will of the dominant class. Its implausibility resides in the claim that the dominant class actually has a cohesive 'will' of which it is conscious.

Marx's theory is fundamentally historicist. That is to say social evolution is explained in terms of inexorable historical forces. Substituting Hegel's dialectical theory of history, Marx and Engels expounded the celebrated concept of 'dialectical materialism'. It is 'materialist' because it claims that the means of production are materially determined; it is 'dialectical', in part, because they predict an inevitable conflict between those two hostile classes, leading to a revolution, as the bourgeois mode of production, based on individual ownership and unplanned competition, stands in contradiction to the increasingly non-individualistic, social character of labour production in the factory. The proletariat, they claim, would seize the means of production and establish a 'dictatorship of the proletariat', to be replaced eventually by a classless, communist society in which law would ultimately be unnecessary.

The law plays an important ideological role. Individuals develop a consciousness of their predicament. Marx famously declared: 'It is not the consciousness of men that determines their being, but, on the contrary, their social being that determines their consciousness.' In other words, our ideas are not arbitrary or fortuitous, they are a result of economic conditions. We absorb our knowledge from our social experience of productive relations. This provides, in part, an explanation of the way in which the law maintains the social order that—as a matter of the 'natural order of things' rather than as a corporately willed desire—represents the interests of the dominant class.

This 'dominant ideology' is tacitly assumed to be the natural order of things through a variety of social institutions. They establish an 'ideological hegemony' which ensures that—educationally, culturally, politically, and legally—this dominant set of values prevails. This explanation first appears in the prison writings of the Italian Marxist Antonio Gramsci and is developed to a high level of sophistication by the French Marxist Louis Althusser.

The Marxist materialist account of law, however, runs into difficulties when governments enact reformist legislation that improves the lot of the working class. How can these laws represent the dominant ideology or interests? One answer given by Marxists is to describe the state as 'relatively autonomous'. It maintains that the capitalist state is not entirely free to act as it pleases in the interests of the ruling class, but is constrained by certain social forces. But it will not permit any fundamental challenge to the capitalist mode of production; it is, at bottom, what Marx and Engels called 'a committee for managing the common affairs of the whole bourgeoisie'.

Since the law is a vehicle of class oppression, it is unnecessary in a classless society. This is the essence of the argument first implied by Marx in his early writings, and reaffirmed by Lenin. In its more sophisticated version, the thesis claims that, following the proletarian revolution, the bourgeois state would be swept aside and replaced by the dictatorship of the proletariat. Society, after reactionary resistance has been overcome, would have no further need for law or state: they would 'wither away'.

One problem with this prognosis is its rather bland equation of law with the coercive suppression of the proletariat. It neglects the fact that a considerable body of law serves other functions and that, even (or especially) a communist society requires laws to plan and regulate the economy. To assert that these are not 'law' is to induce scepticism.

It is important to note that in Marxist legal theory the law is not regarded as anything special. At the core of historical materialism is the proposition that law is 'the result of one particular kind of society' rather than that society is the result of the law. 'Legal fetishism' is the condition, in Balbus's words, where 'individuals affirm that they owe their existence to the Law, rather than the reverse'. Just as there is a form of commodity fetishism, there is a form of legal fetishism which obscures from legal subjects the origins of the legal system's powers and creates the impression that the legal system has a life of its own. Many Marxists spurn the legal fetishism which regards law as a distinct, special, or identifiable phenomenon with its own unique and autonomous form of reasoning and thought.

Equally, they reject not only the concept of justice which, in Marxist terms, is largely dependent upon material conditions, but also the ideal of the rule of law—the notion of law as a neutral body of rules safeguarding freedom. To champion the rule of law would be to accept the image of law as a dispassionate arbiter which is above political conflict and remote from the domination of particular groups or classes. Marxists repudiate this 'consensus' model of society.

The choice between a 'consensus' and 'conflict' model of society is important to our conception of society. Most theories of law, as we have seen, implicitly adopt a consensus view that perceives society as essentially unitary: the legislature represents the common will, the executive acts in the common interest, and the law is a neutral referee that is administered 'without fear or favour' for the common good. There are no fundamental conflicts of values or interests. Any conflicts that arise do so at the personal level: Victoria sues David for damages for breach of contract, and so on.

At the other end of the spectrum is the 'conflict' model which sees society divided between two opposing camps: those who have property and power and those who do not. Conflict is inevitable. The situation of individuals is defined by the very structure of the society: they exist as components of one or other of the two sides. Law in this representation, far from being a neutral referee, is actually the means by which the dominant group maintains its control.

What about human rights? Their ever-increasing significance is clear from Chapter 4. Socialists generally find the very idea of individual rights (and their connotations of selfishness and egoism) incompatible with the communitarian philosophy of Marxism. They therefore explicitly reject the concept and language of rights—except perhaps when their use advances short-term tactical objectives. Their argument is that social change does not occur as a consequence of our moralizing about rights.

Yet in his early writings, Marx maintained that political revolution would end the separation between civil society and the state. Only democratic participation would terminate the alienation of the people from the state. His own vision of socialist rights, or rights under socialism, seems therefore to spring from his denunciation of the distinctive characteristics of a capitalist society: the exploitation and alienation it creates.

Marx distinguishes between 'rights of citizens' and 'rights of man'. The former are political rights exercised in common with others and entail involvement in the community. The latter, on the other hand, are private rights exercised in isolation from others and involve withdrawal from the community. 'Not one of the so-called rights of man', he declares, 'goes beyond egoistic man... an individual withdrawn into himself, his private interests and his private desires'. And, most tellingly, he adds: 'The practical application of the right of man to freedom is the right of man to private property'.

It has been suggested that Marx should not be taken to mean here that these 'rights of man' (equality before the law, security, property, liberty) are not important; but rather that the very concept of such rights is endemic to a society based on capitalist relations of production. This is an awkward contention to sustain, for Marx sought to show that these rights had no independent significance.

Marxists frequently maintain that capitalism is destructive of genuine individual liberty. Private property, according to Marx, represents the dominance of the material world over the human element, while communism represents the triumph of the human element over the material world. He employed the concept of 'reification' to describe the process under which social relations assume the form of relations between things. In a capitalist society, he saw this reification as the result of the alienation of workers from the product of their work: the 'general social form of labour appears as the property of a thing'; it is reified through the 'fetishism of commodities'. Capitalist relations appear to protect individual freedom, but equality before the law is merely a formal property of exchange relations between private property owners.

Revolutionary Marxists reject individual rights mainly because they are an expression of a capitalist economy and will not be required in a classless, socialist society. This rejection rests on four objections to rights:

Their legalism. Rights subject human behaviour to the governance of rules.

Their coerciveness. Law is a coercive device. Rights are tainted for they protect the interests of capital.

Their individualism. They protect self-interested atomized individuals.

Their moralism. They are essentially moral and utopian, and hence irrelevant to the economic base.

But some Marxists regard the view that rights are necessarily individualistic as too crude. The Marxist historian, E. P. Thompson (1924–93), repudiates both the Marxist dismissal of all law as merely an instrument of class rule, and the conception of civil liberties as no more than an illusion which obscures the realities of class rule. He argues that law is not simply an instrument of class domination, but also a 'form of mediation' between and within the classes. Its function is not only to serve power and wealth, but also to impose 'effective inhibitions upon power' and to subject 'the ruling class to its own rules':

> [T]he rule of law itself, the imposing of effective inhibitions upon power and the defence of the citizen from power's all-intrusive claims, seems to me to be an unqualified human good. To deny or belittle this good is, in this dangerous century when the resources and pretensions of power continue to enlarge, a desperate error of intellectual abstraction. More than this, it is a self-fulfilling error, which encourages us to give up the struggle against bad laws and class-bound procedures, and to disarm ourselves before power. It is to throw away a whole inheritance of struggle *about* law, and within

the forms of law, whose continuity can never be fractured without bringing men and women into immediate danger.

Several Marxist writers have, not surprisingly, condemned this wholesale acceptance of the rule of law. Some have argued that to champion restraints on authoritarian rule does not commit Marxists to a comprehensive exaltation of the rule of law.

The collapse of the Soviet Union and its satellite states of Eastern Europe, along with the eclipse of Chinese socialism by state capitalism, has gravely wounded both Marxist legal theory and practice.

Jürgen Habermas

One of the foremost contemporary German intellectuals, Jürgen Habermas (b. 1929) is widely revered for the originality of his philosophy and his perceptive social criticism, though he is not easy reading. Among his numerous insights, which integrate subtle cultural, political, and economic analysis, is his view that despite the inexorable march of 'instrumental-technocratic consciousness', and the domination of the 'lifeworld' it brings in its wake, the capitalist state also presents opportunities for greater 'communicative action'.

The combined effect of capitalism and a strong, centralized authority results, he argues, in the 'lifeworld'—the sphere of common norms and identities—being intruded upon. This generates atomization and alienation (shades of Marx). Because the 'lifeworld' is established by processes whose existence depends on communication and social solidarity, this intrusion undermines the 'lifeworld' itself, and reduces the prospects for collective self-determination. He nevertheless recognizes the prospects for rational communicative discourse in respect of facts, values, and inner experience.

What does this have to do with the law? The answer is complex. Given that his concept of 'communicative reason' is based on the principles of freedom and equality, it would not be unreasonable to expect Habermas to embrace some form of liberalism. In doing so, he distinguishes between 'law as medium' and 'law as institution'. The former describes law as a body of formal, general rules that control the state and the economy. The latter inhabits the 'lifeworld' and hence expresses its shared values and norms in institutional form, for example, those parts of the criminal law that touch on morality. Unlike 'law as medium', 'law as institution' requires legitimation. In fact, argues Habermas, in our pluralistic, fragmented society, these institutions are a potent basis of normative integration.

The legitimacy of the law, he contends, depends significantly on the effectiveness of the process of discourse by which the law is made. Consequently freedom of speech and other fundamental democratic rights are central to his theory of 'communicative action'.

Habermas has provoked a gargantuan literature. He has been criticized, for example, for the disproportionate confidence he places in the law as a vehicle for accomplishing social integration. And some commentators find his suggestion that only those legal norms are valid to which all persons affected have assented as participants in rational discourse somewhat fanciful; he appears to be advocating a form of Athenian democracy!

Michel Foucault

The recondite ideas of influential French thinker Michel Foucault (1926–84) touch, directly and indirectly, on the role of law in society. In particular, his unconventional philosophy, or what, in his later work, he prefers to call 'genealogy', attempts to reveal the nature and function of power. It is, he argues, distinct from either physical force or legal regulation. Nor is it hostile to freedom or truth. Instead, he demonstrates how, beginning in the 18th century, the human body was subjected to a new 'microphysics' of power through the geography of institutions such as factories, hospitals, schools, and prisons.

Discipline consists of four 'practices', each of which engenders consequences on those who are subjected to it. This control creates in those who are its subjects an 'individuality' that contains four characteristics: 'cellular' (by the 'play of spatial distribution'), 'organic' (by the 'coding' of activities), 'genetic' (by the accumulation of time), and 'combinatory' (by the 'composition of forces'). And discipline 'operates four great techniques': it draws up tables, it prescribes movements, it imposes exercises, and it arranges 'tactics' in order to obtain the combination of forces. He concludes:

> Tactics, the art of constructing, with located bodies, coded activities and trained aptitudes, mechanisms in which the product of the various forces is increased by the calculated combination are no doubt the highest form of disciplinary practice.

The application of these methods renders the social order more controllable. Disciplinary power, additionally, induces us to act in ways that we come to think of as natural. We are therefore manipulated and managed by these 'technologies': we become 'docile bodies'—and, as a result, capitalism is able to advance and thrive.

His analysis of power leads him to query liberal ideas, and their preoccupation with centralized state power. Indeed, he regards it as a means by which liberalism actually furthers the very domination it seeks to reduce.

Foucault's universe is one in which disciplinary power pervades almost every element of social life, thus the law has no special claim to primacy. Regulatory government directs policy towards controlling an assortment of threats to the maintenance of social order. The law has thus become 'sociologized'. Formal equality is a smokescreen behind which lies the power that characterizes the postmodern state.

Despite the impenetrability of much of his unsettling work, Foucault's inventive approach to the practice of disciplinary power illuminates the darker reaches of social control by shifting attention away from the institutional operation of the law towards its effect on each of us as individuals.

Chapter 6
Critical legal theory

Many of the theories outlined in the previous five chapters are greeted with scepticism by those who adhere to what, in the broadest sense, may be called critical legal theory. This wing of legal theory generally spurns several of the enterprises that have long been assumed to be at the heart of jurisprudence. And it repudiates what is taken to be the natural order of things, be it patriarchy (in the case of feminist jurisprudence), the conception of 'race' (critical race theory), the free market (critical legal studies), or 'metanarratives' (postmodernism). Each of these spheres of critical thought are briefly examined in this chapter.

The primary purpose of critical legal theory, it is reasonable to assert, is to contest the universal rational foundation of law which, it maintains, clothes the law and legal system with a spurious legitimacy. Nor does critical legal theory accept law as a distinctive and discrete discipline. This view, it alleges, portrays the concept of law as autonomous and determinate—independent from politics and morality—which it can never be.

The myth of determinacy is a significant component of the critical assault on law. Far from being a determinate, coherent body of rules and doctrine, the law is depicted as uncertain, ambiguous, and unstable. And instead of expressing rationality, the law reproduces political and economic power. In addition, as many of the adherents of critical legal studies (CLS) claim, the law is neither neutral nor objective. To achieve neutrality, the law employs several fictions or illusions. Most conspicuously, it vaunts the liberal ideal of equality under the rule of law. But this, in the view of CLS, is a myth. Social justice is a hollow promise.

The movement generated mountainous waves, not only in American law schools, but in their counterparts in Britain, Canada, Australia, and elsewhere. Yet, despite its contemporary chic, CLS is often characterized as a latter-day version of the American realist movement of the 1920s and 1930s. What is 'realism'?

Realism

There are two 'schools' of realism: the American and the Scandinavian. While they share certain similarities, they also differ fundamentally in their approach and methodology, as will become clear later. In particular, although the American movement was largely pragmatist and behaviourist, emphasizing 'law in action' (as opposed to legal conceptualism), the Scandinavians were preoccupied with mounting a philosophical attack on the metaphysical foundations of law. And where the Americans were 'rule-sceptics', the Scandinavians were 'metaphysics-sceptics'. The stronger hostility of the Scandinavians to conceptual thinking about law, especially natural law, may perhaps be explained by the absence of any significant Catholic influence in Scandinavia. Or possibly by the stronger influence of logical positivism in Europe as compared with the United States. The American Realists were immersed in the judicial process, while their Scandinavian counterparts spread their nets more widely to embrace the whole legal system as a whole. Also, the Americans were more empirically minded than the Scandinavians who exhibited an even deeper distrust of metaphysical concepts. Its chief protagonists include Axel Hägerström (1868–1939), Alf Ross (1899–1979), Karl Olivecrona (1897–1980), and A. V. Lundstedt (1882–1955).

Nevertheless the two movements share one significant factor: they reject the conflation of law and morality, and distrust absolute values such as 'justice'. This pragmatism is expressed most vividly in the celebrated maxims of one of the leading exponents of American Realism, Oliver Wendell Holmes, which comes at the end of this striking extract from 'The Path of the Law':

> Take the fundamental question, What constitutes the law? You will find some text writers telling you that it is something different from what is decided by the courts of Massachusetts or England, that it is a system of reason, that it is a deduction from principles of ethics or admitted axioms or whatnot, which may or may not coincide with the decisions. But if we take the view of our friend then we shall find that he does not care two straws for the axioms or deductions, but that he does want to know what the Massachusetts or English courts are likely to do in fact. I am much of his mind. *The prophecies of what the courts will do in fact, and nothing more pretentious, are what I mean by the law.*

Or, as the Scandinavian realist, Alf Ross, put it, to invoke 'justice' is equivalent to banging on a table: it is an emotional expression which turns one's demand into an absolute postulate. 'Realism' is therefore an impatience with theory, a concern with law 'as it is', and a concern with the actual operation of law *in its social context*. To this extent, therefore, legal realism represents an assault on positivism: it is deeply hostile to the formalism that in its view treats law as an inert phenomenon. And yet, realists are—paradoxically—considered to be positivists because of their preoccupation with the law 'as it is' and their almost obsessive pragmatism and empiricism. This chapter concentrates on the American realist movement.

American realism

The Jazz Age generated its jazz jurisprudence. The realists offered a less formalistic, looser account of the 'law in action'. In addition to an intolerance of conceptual 'nonsense', their followers championed a programmatic, educational campaign. But, though they were preoccupied with empirical questions (i.e. attempting to identify the sociological and psychological factors influencing judicial decision-making), their implicit theoretical loyalties were, as stated above, markedly positivist.

Repudiating the naturalist and positivist positions (see Chapters 1 and 2), the movement attached greater importance to political and moral intuitions about the facts of the case. In fact, in the 1930s their frustration with the operation of rules led some to stigmatize realism as nihilistic. Its detractors saw in the movement a rejection not only of morality, but even of legal rules, in the adjudication process. Some critics went so far as to brand realists as anti-democratic and totalitarian.

Their 'core claim', according to Professor Leiter, is that judges respond predominantly to the stimulus of *facts*. Decisions are reached on the basis of a judicial consideration of what seems fair on the facts of the case, rather than on the basis of the applicable legal rule. To understand this claim, Leiter identifies the following three elements:

- In deciding cases, judges react to the underlying facts of the case—whether or not they are legally significant, in other words, whether or not the facts are relevant by virtue of the applicable rules.
- The legal rules and reasons generally have little or no effect, especially in appellate decisions.
- Many of the realists advanced the 'core claim' in the hope of reformulating rules to render them more fact-specific.

The first claim proposes that judicial decisions in indeterminate cases are influenced by the judge's political and moral convictions—not by legal considerations. The second could be said to suggest that the law is indeterminate (along the lines to be pursued by the Critical Legal Studies movement; see later). It suggests that in the majority of appellate decisions, the available legal materials are insufficient to produce a unique legal outcome.

Among the movement's leading members, three stand out: Oliver Wendell Holmes, Karl N. Llewellyn, and Jerome Frank. Holmes (1841–1935) was the intellectual, and perhaps even the spiritual, father of American Realism. 'The common law,' he famously declared, 'is not a brooding omnipresence in the sky, but the articulate voice of some sovereign or quasi sovereign that can be identified...'

The central contribution of Karl Llewellyn was his functionalism. This approach perceives law as serving certain fundamental functions: 'law-jobs'. We should, he argues, regard law as an engine 'having purposes, not values in itself'. If society is to survive, certain basic needs must be satisfied; this engenders conflict which must be resolved. Six 'law-jobs' are identified:

1. Adjustment of trouble cases.
2. Preventive channelling of conduct and expectations.
3. Preventive rechannelling of conduct and expectations to adjust to change.
4. Allocation of authority and determination of procedures for authoritative decision-making.
5. Provision of direction and incentive within the group.
6. 'The job of the juristic method'.

What are realists 'realist' about?

1. The conception of *law in flux*, of moving law, and of judicial creation of law.
2. The conception of law *as a means to social ends*, and not as an end in itself.

3. The conception of *society in flux*—faster than law.
4. The *temporary divorce of 'is' and 'ought' for the purpose of study.*
5. *Distrust of traditional legal rules and concepts* as descriptive of what courts or people actually do.
6. *Distrust of the theory that traditional prescriptive rule formulations are the main factor* in producing court decisions.
7. The belief in grouping cases and legal situations into *narrower categories.*
8. An insistence on evaluating the law in terms of its *effects.*
9. An insistence on *sustained and programmatic attack* on the problems of law.

Karl Llewellyn, 'Some Realism about Realism', *Harvard Law Review* 44 (1931): 1222

This functionalist account of law stresses the 'institution' of law which performs various jobs: an institution is, for Llewellyn, an organized activity built around the doing of a job or cluster of jobs. And the most important job the law has is the disposition of trouble cases; law is a 'technology' rather than a 'philosophy'. As well as major institutions (which are concerned with essential jobs or job clusters upon which the existence of society depends), there are also minor institutions such as crafts. These consist of the skills that are held by a body of specialists; the practice of the law is a craft.

Llewellyn drew a famous distinction between the grand style and the formal style of judicial opinions. The former is 'the style of reason' which is informed by 'policy' considerations, while the latter is logical and formal and seeks refuge in rules of law. He, needless to say, preferred the grand style and the 'situation sense' which is its hallmark. His argument is not that either of these styles is to be found in pure form. Instead, he describes a situation in which there is an oscillation between the two. Thus, in the early part of the 19th century, when American law was at its creative height, the grand style was deployed. From the middle of the 19th century, however, Llewellyn detects a shift toward the formal style. In the middle of the 20th century, he finds evidence of a swing back to the grand style, a development he applauds as 'the best device ever invented by man for drying up that free-flowing spring of uncertainty, conflict between the seeming commands of the authorities and the felt demands of justice'.

Jerome Frank (1889–1957) is generally associated with the distinction he drew between 'rule-sceptics' (who include Llewellyn, and who, he said, were afflicted with 'appellate court-itis') and 'fact-sceptics' (among whom he counted himself), who were concerned to reveal the unconscious forces that affect the discovery and interpretation of the *facts* of the case. For Frank, most realists, in their preoccupation with appellate courts, missed the important aspect of randomness and unpredictability in the judicial process: the elusiveness of *facts*. Thus the various prejudices of judges and jurors ('for example, plus or minus reactions to women, or unmarried women, or red-haired women, or brunettes, or men with deep voices, or fidgety men, or men who wear thick eyeglasses, or those who have pronounced gestures or nervous tics') frequently affect the outcome of a case. The main thrust of Frank's attack was directed against the idea that certainty could be achieved through legal rules. If it were so, he argued, why would anyone bother to litigate? Even where there is an applicable rule, one of two opposite conclusions is possible. We *want* the law to be certain, he suggested, because of our deep need for security and safety which is prevalent among children. In the same way as a child places his trust in the wisdom of his father, so we seek in the law and other institutions a similar comforting security.

American Realism is informed by a behaviourist view of law that is evident in all the leading members of the movement.

Behaviourism attempts to describe and explain the *outward manifestations* of mental processes and other phenomena that are not directly observable and measurable. Thus behavioural psychology is concerned principally with the measurement of legal, and particularly judicial, *behaviour*. And this is especially evident in the realists' near-obsession with 'prediction'. The movement has attracted charges of 'naive realism', 'barefoot empiricism' and, most recently, 'pragmatic instrumentalism', and 'profound conservatism'.

The realist challenge to the autonomy of law was undoubtedly an important precursor of the critical legal studies and postmodernist approaches to law and the legal system discussed later in this chapter. The relationship between the realist movement and sociological jurisprudence is also a strong one (see Chapter 5).

There has been something of a re-evaluation of American Realism undertaken by Brian Leiter who challenges the view that realism is a 'jurisprudential joke, a tissue of philosophical confusions'. He maintains that 'it is time for legal philosophers to stop treating Realism as a discredited historical antique, and start looking at the movement with the sympathetic eye it deserves'.

Critical legal studies

CLS emerged in the 1970s in the United States as a broadly leftist critique of orthodox legal doctrines. Originally, it had three typical features. It was situated within legal, as opposed to political science or sociological scholarship. Second, it sought to challenge the injustices it identified in legal doctrine. And, third, it adopted an interdisciplinary approach, drawing on politics, philosophy, literary criticism, psychoanalysis, linguistics, and semiotics to explain its critique of law.

While it is true that both American Realism and CLS share a sceptical, anti-formalist view, CLS cannot properly be regarded as a 'new realism'. Though both movements seek to demystify the law, and to expose its operation as law 'in action', CLS does not engage in the pragmatic or empirical concerns that preoccupied the realists. Instead, its adherents regard the law as 'problematic' in the sense that it reproduces the oppressive nature of society. Moreover, unlike the American realists who accepted the division between legal reasoning and politics, CLS regards it as axiomatic that, in effect, law *is* politics; and legal reasoning is no different from other forms of reasoning. In addition, although the realists sought to distinguish between legal rules and their actual operation in society, they generally embraced the neutrality of law and the ideology of liberalism. CLS denies both.

Indeed, applying Marxist and Freudian ideas, CLS detects in the law a form of 'hegemonic consciousness', a term borrowed from the writings of the Italian Marxist, Antonio Gramsci, who observed that social order is maintained by a system of beliefs which are accepted as 'common sense' and part of the natural order—even by those who are actually subordinated to it. In other words, these ideas are treated as eternal and necessary whereas they really reflect only the transitory, arbitrary interests of the dominant elite.

And they are 'reified', a term used by Marx and refined by the Hungarian Marxist, György Lukács, to refer to the manner in which ideas become material things, and are portrayed as essential, necessary, and objective when, in fact, they are contingent, arbitrary, and subjective. Moreover, legal thought is, following Freud, a form of 'denial': it affords a way of coping with contradictions that are too painful for us to hold in our conscious mind. It therefore denies the contradiction between the promise, on the one hand of, say, equality and freedom, and the reality of oppression and hierarchy, on the other.

The Brazilian social theorist, Roberto Unger (b. 1947), is an important source of CLS ideas. The representation of society, he contends, is infused with the following four beliefs. First, that law is a 'system', and as a body of 'doctrine', properly interpreted, it supplies the answer to all questions about social behaviour. Second, that a special form of legal reasoning exists by which answers may be found from doctrine. Third, that this doctrine reflects a coherent view about the relations between persons and the nature of society. And, fourth, that social action reflects norms generated by the legal system, either because people internalize these norms or actual coercion compels them to do so.

CLS challenges each of these assumptions. First, it denies that law is a system or is able to resolve every conceivable problem. This is described as the principle of *indeterminacy*. Second, it rejects the view that there is an autonomous and neutral mode of legal reasoning. This is described as the principle of *anti-formalism*. Third, it contests the view that doctrine encapsulates a single, coherent view of human relations; instead CLS maintains that doctrine represents several different, often opposing points of view, none of which is sufficiently coherent or pervasive to be called dominant. This is described as the principle of *contradiction*. Finally, it doubts that, even where there is consensus, there is reason to regard the law as a decisive factor in social behaviour. This is described as the principle of *marginality*.

If law is indeterminate, legal scholarship defining what the law is becomes merely a form of advocacy. If there is no distinct form of legal reasoning, such scholarship is reduced to political debate. If legal doctrine is essentially contradictory, legal argument cannot rely on it, if it is not to result in a draw. And if law is marginal, social life must be controlled by norms exterior to the law.

Some of the more radical ideas of CLS are difficult to take seriously. The suggestion, for example, that to counter the hierarchy endemic to law schools, all its employees—from professors to janitors—be paid the same salary has not been enthusiastically endorsed, at least by the former group. There is no question, however, that CLS has played a significant role in illuminating the fissure between rhetoric and reality. Yet the possibilities of transforming the law seem frequently to be diluted by the destructive, even nihilistic, tendencies of some of the more dogmatic adherents of CLS. Many of its ideas are still influential in the legal academy, though they have been absorbed, adapted, and refined by the theories that occupy the remainder of this chapter.

Postmodern legal theory

'I define *postmodern* as incredulity toward metanarratives.' Thus spake Jean-François Lyotard (1924–98) in his influential book, *The Postmodern Condition: A Report on Knowledge*. The promise of truth or justice held out by the grand 'metanarratives' of Kant, Hegel, Marx, and others has, in our age, been betrayed. Universal values, 'master narratives', are regarded by postmodernists like Lyotard as superfluous, if not meaningless. The great historical epochs, developments, and ideas, especially those associated with the Enlightenment—and the Enlightenment itself—are treated with profound suspicion. The conventional assumption that human 'progress' is 'evolving' towards 'civilization' or some other end is rejected by postmodernists who seek interpretation and understanding in the personal experience of individuals.

This attack on the Enlightenment includes a dismissal of the Kantian concern with individual rights, equality, and justice characteristic of modernism. But the target is even larger, for the espousal of these values is not confined to those who champion the idea of natural rights (see Chapter 1). They are adopted by a good deal of post-Enlightenment legal theory, including positivism (see Chapter 2). Drawing on elements of 'cultural theory', and the writings of Michel Foucault (see Chapter 5), Jacques Derrida, Jacques Lacan (see later), and other—principally French and German—theorists, postmodernism may also be understood as an attempt to invalidate, or at least to contest, the methods, assumptions, and ideas of the analytical Anglo-American philosophical tradition.

Postmodernist accounts of society, and the role of law within it, disclose a disillusionment with formalism, essentialism, statism, utopianism, and even democracy. Nor does the scepticism end here. Critical theory, whether aesthetic or ethical, seeks to subvert 'foundational' ideas of truth. It expresses an impatience with the modern state's bureaucratic suffocation of the individual, the overarching presence of the state, the increasing globalization of markets, and universalizing of values.

It has also (perhaps inevitably) witnessed a new pragmatism. A down-to-earth set of goals—economic, ecological, political—is accompanied by the advocacy of a more inclusive community that emphasizes the special predicament of women, minorities, the dispossessed, and the poor. A popular expression (to be found also among CLS and feminist theorists) is 'empowerment'. But the radical postmodern political agenda is a complex one which may generate confusion or what has been called a 'multiplication of ideologies'.

Both the 'subject' and the 'object' are regarded as fantasies. And the postmodern concern with the 'subject' generates, especially in the context of the law, some fascinating accounts of the individual as moral agent, as rights-bearer, or simply as player in the legal system. Several are explicitly psychological or linguistic, with the structural psychoanalytical theories of Lacan and the poststructuralist ideas of Derrida exerting considerable influence, though, as will be suggested below, they have little utility in our quest to comprehend the nature of law.

Jacques Lacan

The French psychoanalyst, Jacques Lacan (1901–81), is frequently described as the architect of postmodern psychoanalytic semiotics.

Drawing on the ideas of Freud, Saussure, and Lévi-Strauss, he argues that the unconscious is structured like a language; it is therefore crucial to identify the inner workings of that discourse that takes place within the unconscious—the repository of knowledge, power, agency, and desire. We do not control what we say; rather the structure of language is predetermined by thought and desire. He employs a psychoanalytical, Freudian conception of the divided human subject—ego, superego, and the unconscious—to demonstrate that the 'I' expressed by language (which he calls the 'subject of the statement') can never represent an individual's 'true' identity (which he calls the 'subject of enunciation').

In the first 18 months of our lives we experience this disjunction between identity and its representation, and thereafter it is forever lost. We construct a semblance of individual and social stability only by fantasy, which cannot be sustained. The subject is thus divided or decentred. The language of the unconscious is the arbiter of all experience, knowing, and living. The idea of justice becomes, in Lacanian terms, a fantasy that camouflages the unattainable desire of a harmonious community.

Jacques Derrida

The controversial French philosopher Jacques Derrida (1930–2004) is closely associated with the concept of deconstruction. He employs the term—which he borrowed from the German philosopher, Martin Heidegger—to explicate the notion of *différance*. This neologism describes the state of interdependence and difference between hierarchical oppositions. 'Difference' is based on the French word *différer*, which means both to differ and to defer. He replaces an 'e' with the 'a' in *différance*. The words are indistinguishable in spoken French.

Based on the semiotics of the Swiss linguist, Ferdinand de Saussure, Derrida draws a distinction between 'signifiers' and 'signified'. Saussure distinguished between *langue*, the deep structure of linguistic rules, and *parole*, the set of speech acts made by members of a linguistic community. The former is, in the understanding of language, the more important element because it is the system of relations among various signs that constitutes a language. So, for example, the word 'dog' does not correspond to the creature we know and love. But we understand it by virtue of its difference from similar sounds such as 'bog', 'cog', or 'fog'. Derrida postulates that, since the meaning of 'dog' emerges from this contest of differences between signifiers, its meaning—like the meaning of all signifiers—is infinitely deferred. He concludes that stability can be achieved only by 'deconstructing' language in order to show how the meaning of one signifier includes within it another signifier (the 'other').

Derrida's undertaking is ambitious: to expose the 'metaphysics of presence' in Western philosophy. By this he means that, in every set of oppositions, one kind of 'presence' is privileged over a corresponding kind of 'absence'. Western philosophy, he argues, is based on the hidden premise that what is most apparent to our consciousness—what is obvious or immediate—is most real, foundational, or important.

Derrida's disquieting deduction is that, since language emerges from this unstable structure of differences, it will always be indeterminate. The prospect of establishing the subject of identity—and hence of an individual right-holder—is consequently poor.

Though postmodern legal theory has garnered a sizeable following, one is bound to question whether it greatly assists our understanding of law. How, for example, can deconstruction provide a constructive insight into the concept of law? Since, as we have seen, the legitimacy of the law lies in some conception of justice, and the language of the law is unavoidably normative, it is hard to see how Lacanian psychoanalysis or Derrida's deconstruction advance our comprehension of legal ideas.

Feminist legal theory

Traditional jurisprudence conspicuously overlooked the position of women. Feminist legal theory has been remarkably successful in remedying this neglect. It has had a considerable impact, not only on university law curricula, but on the law itself, for feminist jurisprudence extends well beyond the purely academic to comprehensive analysis of the many inequalities to be found in the criminal law, especially rape and domestic violence, family law, contract, tort, property, and other branches of the substantive law, including aspects of public law.

In recent years, for example, both English and American courts have abandoned the common law principle that a husband cannot be prosecuted for raping his wife, despite her refusal to consent to sexual intercourse. The wife was deemed by the fact of marriage to have consented. While the judges make no explicit reference to feminist jurisprudence, its influence may well have played a part in these decisions.

Not surprisingly, in view of its unease about the injustices experienced by women, feminist writing is often overtly polemical. 'The personal is political' was the compelling slogan adopted by early feminists. It represented in part a denunciation of the professed radicalism of social movements that failed to address the routine subjugation of women at home or at work.

Nor, of course, do feminists speak with a single voice. There are at least five major strands of legal feminism. What follows is an outline of their diverse perspectives, as well as a summary of the achievements of the feminist movement in theory and practice.

Liberal feminism

Liberalism prizes individual rights, both civil and political. Liberals assert the need for a large realm of personal freedom, including freedom of speech, conscience, association, and sexuality, immune to state regulation, save to protect others from harm. Liberal feminism perceives individuals as autonomous, rights-bearing agents, and stresses the values of equality, rationality, and autonomy. Since men and women are equally rational, it is argued, they ought to have the same opportunities to exercise rational choices. (This emphasis on equality, as we shall see, is stigmatized by radical feminists as mistaken, because asserting women's similarity to men assimilates women into the male domain, thereby making women into men.)

The majority of liberal feminists, while conceding that the legal and political system is patriarchal, refuse to accept the blanket assault that is a significant, though not universal, item on the radical agenda. The liberal battleground is the existing institutional framework of discrimination, particularly in the domain of employment.

Liberal feminism accentuates equality, while radical feminism is concerned with difference. Among the most critical anxieties of liberal feminists is the border between the private and the public domain. This is largely because women tend to be excluded from the public sphere where political equality is realized. Likewise, the private domain of the home and office is the site of the subordination and exploitation of women. Crimes of domestic violence normally occur within the home into which the law is often reluctant to intrude. Liberalism may itself therefore be implicated in the subjugation of women, according to radical feminists.

Radical feminism

Leading radical feminist Catharine MacKinnon (b. 1946) contests the idea that, since men have defined women as different, women can ever achieve equality. Given that men dominate women, she argues that the question is ultimately one of power. The law is effectively a masculine edifice that cannot be altered merely by admitting women through its doors or including female values within its rules or procedures. Nor, the radical position contends, is reforming the law likely to assist since, in view of the masculinity of law, it will simply produce male oriented results and reproduce male dominated relations. In the words of MacKinnon: 'Abstract rights... authorize the male experience of the world.'

Radical feminism rejects what it regards as the liberal illusion of the neutrality of the law. It seeks to expose the reality behind the mask so that women will recognize the need to change the patriarchal system which subjugates them.

The differences—or dualisms—between the genders, according to Frances Olsen, are 'sexualized'. Masculine characteristics are considered superior.

Carol Smart denies that the law can produce real equality. Ann Scales is eloquent in her dismissal of change through the form of law:

> We should be especially wary when we hear lawyers, addicted to cognitive objectivity as they are, assert that women's voices have a place in the existing system.... The injustice of sexism is not irrationality; it is domination. Law must focus on the latter, and that focus cannot be achieved through a formal lens.

Christine Littleton advocates 'equality as acceptance', which emphasizes the consequences rather than the sources of difference, an approach that has obvious legal consequences in respect of equal pay and conditions of work.

Radical feminism seeks to expose the domination of women by 'asking the woman question' to expose the gender implications of rules and practices that might otherwise appear to be impartial or neutral.

The differences—or dualisms—between the genders, according to Frances Olsen, are 'sexualized'. Masculine characteristics are considered superior.

MALE	FEMALE
Rational	Irrational
Active	Passive
Thought	Feeling
Reason	Emotion
Culture	Nature
Power	Sensitivity
Objective	Subjective
Abstract	Contextualized

(Adapted from Frances Olsen, 'Feminism and Critical Legal Theory: An American Perspective, *International Journal of the Sociology of Law* 18 (1990): 199)

Postmodern feminism

Postmodernists, we have seen, generally reject the idea of the 'subject'. And they exhibit an impatience with objective truths such as 'equality', 'gender', 'the law', 'patriarchy', and even 'woman'. Indeed, the very idea that things have properties which they must possess if they are to be that particular thing (i.e. that they have 'essences') is repudiated by many postmodernists. This 'essentialism' is discerned by postmodern feminists in the approach of radical feminists such as Catharine MacKinnon who argues that below the surface of women lies 'precultural woman'.

Drucilla Cornell and Frances Olsen draw on the work of Jacques Derrida and Julia Kristeva to construct what Cornell calls an 'imaginative universal' which transcends the essentialism of real experience and enters the realm of mythology. The maleness of law—the 'phallocentrism' of society—is a central theme in postmodern feminist writing. Katherine Bartlett identifies at least three feminist legal methods that are used in investigating the legal process: 'asking the woman question', 'feminist practical reasoning', and 'consciousness-raising'. The first attempts to expose the gender implications of rules and practices that may appear to be neutral. The second, feminist practical reasoning, challenges the legitimacy of the norms that, through rules, claim to represent the community, especially in cases of rape and domestic violence cases. And the third, consciousness-raising seeks to understand and reveal women's oppression.

Difference feminism

Difference (or cultural) feminism is uncomfortable with the liberal feminists' attachment to formal equality and gender. This position, it maintains, undermines the differences between men and women. Instead, difference feminism endeavours to reveal the unstated premises of the law's substance, practice, and procedure by exposing the miscellaneous kinds of discrimination implicit in the criminal law, the law of evidence, tort law, and the process of legal reasoning itself. This includes an attack on, for example, the concept of the 'reasonable man', the male view of female sexuality applied in rape cases, and the very language of the law itself.

It argues that equality is a more subtle and complex objective than liberals allow. Thus Carol Gilligan, a psychologist, demonstrates how women's moral values tend to stress responsibility, whereas men emphasize rights. Women look to context, where men appeal to neutral, abstract notions of justice. In particular, she argues, women endorse an 'ethic of care' which proclaims that no one should be hurt. This morality of caring and nurturing identifies and defines an essential difference between the sexes.

Difference feminism focuses upon the positive characteristic of women's 'special bond' to others, while radical feminism concentrates on the negative dimension: the sexual objectification of women, through, for example, pornography, which MacKinnon describes as 'a form of forced sex'.

Critical race theory

CRT originated in Madison, Wisconsin, in 1989 as a reaction against what it saw as the deconstructive excesses of CLS. Nevertheless, it is no less sceptical of Enlightenment ideas such as 'justice', 'truth', and 'reason'. Its mainspring, however, is the need to expose the law's pervasive racism; privileged white, middle-class academics, in its view, cannot fully uncover its nature and extent. Those who have themselves suffered the indignity and injustice of discrimination are the authentic voices of marginalized racial minorities. The law's formal constructs reflect, it is argued, the reality of a privileged, elite, male, white majority. It is this culture, way of life, attitude, and normative behaviour that combine to form the prevailing 'neutrality' of the law. A racial minority is condemned to the margins of legal existence.

CRT diverges most radically from full-blown postmodernist accounts (see earlier) in respect of the recognition by at least some of its members of the importance of conventional 'rights talk' in pursuit of

The end of consensus?

'While critical legal scholars have attacked the quest for consensus which has dominated post-realist American jurisprudence, their transformative agenda, feminists and critical race theorists argue, betrays their faith in the possibility of a society founded on some sort of alternative consensus. Yet this new society, with its alternative consensus, would not necessarily fare any better than does liberal legalism in accommodating the experiences, values and concerns of women and minority groups. Taken together, feminist jurisprudence and critical race theory may be read as a call for an end to the quest for consensus.'

N. Duxbury, *Patterns of American Jurisprudence*, p. 509

equality and freedom. Its analysis of society and law therefore seems, in some cases, to be a partial one. This retreat from the postmodernist antagonism towards rights signifies an apparent readiness to embrace the ideals of liberty, equality, and justice. Several CRT adherents, however, evince profound misgivings about liberalism and the formal equality it aspires to protect, and a distaste for individual rights and other contents of the liberal package.

CRT scholarship often draws on 'auto/biography' to appraise social and legal relations. Patricia Williams, for example,

12. The American civil rights movement of the 1960s ultimately achieved its principal objective of racial equality under the law

amalgamates legal analysis and personal narrative to criticize legal subjectivity. CRT regards the hostility of traditional legal scholarship to the auto/biographical as a method by which to distance the law from the very social relations, especially racial and gender discrimination, that it generates (see Figure 12).

An offshoot of CRT pursues the postcolonial thesis that the dismantling of colonial governments has failed to end the racial divisions and assumptions of these societies.

Chapter 7

Understanding law: a very short epilogue

This book began with a number of questions. What is law? Does it consist of universal moral values in accordance with nature? Or is law merely a collection of predominantly man-made rules, commands, or norms? Does the law have a specific purpose such as justice, the protection of individual rights, or economic, political, gender, and racial equality? Can the law be understood without a proper appreciation of its social context? And these are merely some of the concerns of legal philosophy. What of unjust laws: do we have an obligation to obey them? How do we justify punishing offenders? How can the law better protect the environment, the handicapped, and animals?

These—and a myriad related—subjects animate much of contemporary legal theory. The seemingly intractable problem of the relationship between law and morals continues to dominate academic debate. Can law be as neutral and value-free as legal positivists seek to demonstrate, or is law steeped in inescapable moral values? Can law be analytically severed from morality? Or is the pursuit of neutrality and objectivity by legal positivists—from Austin and Bentham to the Realists and their modern followers—a sanguine will o' the wisp? Is a 'science of law' (exemplified by Kelsen's 'Pure Theory') a chimera? Is Hart's focus upon the 'municipal legal system' still helpful in our age of globalization and pluralism? If law does have a purpose, what might it be? Can it secure greater justice for all who share our troubled planet?

None of these questions has a simple answer. But it is in their asking—and careful reflection upon them—that we might better understand the nature and purpose of law, and thereby perhaps secure a more just society. Is this not ample justification for legal philosophy?

References

Chapter 1: Natural Law

A. Passerin D'Entrèves, *Natural Law: An Introduction to Legal Philosophy*, 2nd edn (London: Hutchinson, 1970), p. 116.

J. Finnis, *Natural Law and Natural Rights*, 2nd edn (Oxford: Clarendon Press, 2002), pp. 3, 34.

Cicero, *De Re Publica*, trans. C. W. Keyes (London: William Heinemann, 1928) (Loeb Classical Library), 3.22.33.

St Augustine, *City of God*, trans. W. C. Greene (London: William Heinemann, 1960) (Loeb Classical Library), 4.4.

St Thomas Aquinas, *Summa Theologiae* in *Selected Political Writings* trans. J. G. Dawson, ed. A. Passerin D'Entrèves (Oxford: Basil Blackwell, 1970 reprint of 1959 edn), I/II.96.4.

'It is often supposed...' J. Finnis, *Natural Law and Natural Rights*, 2nd edn (Oxford: Oxford University Press, 2011), p. 3.

'There is, I think, no alternative...' J. Finnis, *Natural Law and Natural Rights*, 2nd edn (Oxford: Oxford University Press, 2011), pp. 219–20, emphasis added.

'The war between anti-abortion groups...' R. Dworkin, *Life's Dominion: An Argument about Abortion and Euthanasia* (London: HarperCollins, 1993), p. 4.

Roe v. Wade 410 US 113, 93 S. Ct. 705, 35 L. Ed. 2d 147 (1973).

'He lies in...hospital...fed liquid food...' *Airedale NHS Trust v. Bland* [1993] AC 789 at 824–5 *per* Hoffmann L. J. (as he then was).

Cruzan v. Director, Missouri Department of Health, 497 U.S. 261 (1990).

S. J. Shapiro, *Legality* (Cambridge, MA: Belknap Press of Harvard University Press, 2011).

Chapter 2: Legal positivism

'[T]he certification of something as legally valid...' H. L. A. Hart, *The Concept of Law*, 3nd edn with introduction and notes by L. Green, and postscript ed. J. Raz, and P. A. Bulloch (Oxford: Clarendon Press, 2012), pp. 57, 210, 117.

'The assertion that a legal system exists...' H. L. A. Hart, *The Concept of Law*, 3nd edn with introduction and notes by L. Green, and postscript ed. J. Raz, and P. A. Bulloch (Oxford: Clarendon Press, 2012), p. 113.

'What is necessary is that there should be...' H. L. A. Hart, *The Concept of Law*, 3nd edn with introduction and notes by L. Green, and postscript ed. J. Raz, and P. A. Bulloch (Oxford: Clarendon Press, 2012), p. 56.

'Coercive acts ought to be performed...' H. Kelsen, *Pure Theory of Law* (Berkeley, CA: University of California Press, 1967), pp. 115–16.

J. Raz *The Authority of Law* (Oxford: Oxford University Press, 1979), pp. 37 ff.

Chapter 3: Dworkin: the moral integrity of law

'He knows that other judges...' R. Dworkin, *Law's Empire* (Cambridge, MA: Harvard University Press, 1986), p. 239.

'[L]aw as integrity accepts law...' R. Dworkin, *Law's Empire* (Cambridge, MA: Harvard University Press, 1986), pp. 95–6, emphasis added.

'because the proposition that...' R. Dworkin, *Justice for Hedgehogs* (Cambridge, MA: The Belknap Press of Harvard University Press, 2011), p. 17, emphasis added.

'Someone lives well when he senses...' R. Dworkin, *Justice for Hedgehogs* (Cambridge, MA: The Belknap Press of Harvard University Press, 2011), p. 17.

R. Dworkin, *Taking Rights Seriously*, New impression with a reply to critics (London: Duckworth, 1978), pp. 116–17.

Chapter 4: Rights and justice

W. N. Hohfeld, *Fundamental Legal Conceptions as Applied in Judicial Reasoning*, ed. W. W. Cook (New Haven, CN, and London: Yale University Press, 1964).

'It would be... wrong...' R. Dworkin, *Justice for Hedgehogs* (Cambridge, MA: The Belknap Press, 2011), p. 224.

'The term 'human right' is nearly criterionless' J. Griffin, *On Human Rights* (Oxford: Oxford University Press, 2008), pp. 14–15.
'there is an irreducible diversity...' J. Ladd, 'Introduction', in J. Ladd (ed.), *Ethical Relativism* (Belmont, CA: Wadsworth, 1973), 2.
'I have tried to develop a moral theory...' R. Posner, *The Economics of Justice* (Cambridge, MA: Harvard University Press, 1981), p. 115.
'The common law method...' R. Posner, *The Economic Analysis of Law*, 2nd edn (Boston, MA: Little, Brown, 1977), p. 179.
'To the extent that people conceal...' R. Posner, 'The Right of Privacy', *Georgia Law Review* (1978): 393, 401.
Justinian, *Corpus Juris Civilis*. The first quotation is from book 1, title 1, paragraph 10 of Justinian's Digest. The second is from the same source, book 1, title 2. The author is Ulpian. The translations are mine.
J. Bentham, *An Introduction to the Principles of Morals and Legislation*, in J. H. Burns and H. L. A. Hart (eds), *The Collected Works of Jeremy Bentham* (London: Athlone Press, 1970; general editor, J. H. Burns, chap. 1, para 1.
The desert island example is adapted from Nigel Simmonds, *Central Issues in Jurisprudence*, 3rd edn (London: Sweet & Maxwell, 2008), p. 26.
The four criticisms are expressed by H. L. A. Hart, 'Between Utility and Rights', *Essays in Jurisprudence and Philosophy* (Oxford: Clarendon Press, 1982), pp. 200–2.

Chapter 5: Law and society

'integration of all analytically derived...' *Max Weber on Law in Economy and Society*, ed. M. Rheinstein, trans. E. Shils and M. Rheinstein (Cambridge, MA: Harvard University Press, 1954; 20th Century Legal Philosophy Series), Vol. 6, pp. 5, 62.
M. Weber, *The Religion of China: Confucianism and Taoism*, trans. and ed. H. H. Gerth (Glencoe, IL: The Free Press, 1951), p. 149.
Max Weber on Law in Economy and Society, ed. M. Rheinstein, trans. E. Shils and M. Rheinstein (Cambridge, MA: Harvard University Press, 1954; 20th Century Legal Philosophy Series), Vol. 6, p. 225.
'Legal fetishism...' I am here paraphrasing Balbus, 'Commodity Form and Legal Form: An Essay on the "Relative Autonomy of the Law"', *Law and Society Review* 11 (1977): 582.
K. Marx, 'On the Jewish Question', in D. McLellan (ed.), *Karl Marx: Selected Writings* (Oxford: Oxford University Press, 1977).

'[T]he rule of law itself…' E. P. Thompson, *Whigs and Hunters* (Harmondworth: Penguin, 1975), p. 266.

'Tactics, the art of constructing…' M. Foucault, *Discipline and Punish*, tr. A. Sheridan (Harmondsworth: Penguin, 1977), p. 167.

Chapter 6: Critical legal theory

'Take the fundamental question…' O. W. Holmes Jr, (1897) 10 *Harvard Law Review* 460–1, emphasis added.

'If you want to know the law…' O. W. Holmes Jr, *Collected Legal Papers*, p. 171, quoted by W. Twining, *Karl Llewellyn and the Realist Movement* (London: Weidenfeld & Nicholson, 1973), p. 17.

'Their "core claim"…' B. Leiter, *Naturalizing Jurisprudence: Essays on American Legal Realism and Naturalism in Legal Philosophy* (Oxford: Oxford University Press, 2007).

K. Llewellyn, 'A Realistic Jurisprudence—The Next Step' *Columbia Law Review* (1930): 431.

K. Llewellyn, *The Common Law Tradition: Deciding Appeals* (Boston, MA: Little, Brown & Co., 1960).

'four beliefs…' these are described by David Trubek, 'CLS and Empiricism: Where the Action Is' in a symposium published in *Stanford Law Review* 36 (1984): 413.

Marital rape cases: *R v. R* [1992] 1 AC 599, House of Lords; *Smith v. Smith* 85 NJ 193, 426 A 2d 38 (1981).

'We should be especially wary…' A. Scales, 'The Emergence of Feminist Jurisprudence: An Essay', *Yale Law Journal* 95 (1986): 1373, 1385.

K. Bartlett, 'Feminist Legal Method', *Harvard Law Review* 103 (1990): 829.

R. Delgado and J. Stefanic, 'Critical Race Theory: An Annotated Bibliography', *Virginia Law Review* 79 (1993): 461.

Further reading

Chapter 1: Natural law

Finnis, J., *Natural Law and Natural Rights* (2nd edn, Oxford: Clarendon Press, 2011).

—— (ed.), *Natural Law* (in 2 vols, Aldershot: Dartmouth, 1991).

—— 'Natural Law: The Classical Tradition', in Jules Coleman and Scott Shapiro (eds), *The Oxford Handbook of Jurisprudence and Philosophy of Law* (Oxford: Oxford University Press, 2002).

Fuller, L. L., *The Morality of Law* (rev. edn, Yale: Yale University Press, 1969).

George, Rt P., *In Defense of Natural Law* (Oxford: Oxford University Press, 1999).

—— *Conscience and its Enemies: Confronting the Dogmas of Liberal Secularism* (London: ISI Books, 2013).

Passerin D'Entrèves, A., *Natural Law: An Introduction to Legal Philosophy* (2nd edn, London: Hutchinson, 1970).

Chapter 2: Legal positivism

Austin, J., *The Province of Jurisprudence Determined and the Uses of the Study of Jurisprudence* (London: Weidenfeld & Nicolson, 1954).

Bentham, J., *A Fragment on Government; or, A Comment on the Commentaries* (2nd edn, London: W. Pickering, 1823).

—— *An Introduction to the Principles of Morals and Legislation*, ed. J. H. Burns and H. L. A. Hart (London: Athlone Press, 1970).

Bentham, J., *Of Laws in General*, ed. H. L. A. Hart (London: Athlone Press, 1970).
Coleman, J. (ed.), *Hart's Postscript: Essays on the Postscript to The Concept of Law* (Oxford: Oxford University Press, 2001).
—— *The Practice of Principle: In Defence of A Pragmatic Approach to Legal Theory* (Oxford: Oxford University Press, 2001).
George, Robert P. (ed.), *The Autonomy of Law: Essays on Legal Positivism* (Oxford: Clarendon Press, 1995).
Hart, H. L. A., *Essays on Bentham: Studies on Jurisprudence and Political Theory* (Oxford: Clarendon Press, 1982).
—— *The Concept of Law* (3nd edn with introduction and notes by L. Green, and postscript ed. J. Raz, and P. A. Bulloch, Oxford: Clarendon Press, 2012).
Himma, K. E. 'Inclusive Legal Positivism', in Jules Coleman and Scott Shapiro (eds), *The Oxford Handbook of Jurisprudence and Philosophy of Law* (Oxford: Oxford University Press, 2002).
Jori, M. (ed.), *Legal Positivism* (Aldershot: Dartmouth: The International Library of Jurisprudence, 1992).
Kelsen, H., *General Theory of Law and State*, trans. Anders Wedberg (Cambridge, MA: Harvard University Press, 1949).
—— *Pure Theory of Law*, trans. M. Knight (California: University of California Press, 1967).
—— *General Theory of Norms*, trans. M. Hartney (Oxford: Clarendon Press, 1991).
—— *Introduction to the Problems of Legal Theory*, trans. B. Litschewski Paulson and S. L. Paulson (Oxford: Clarendon Press, 1992).
Kramer, M., *In Defense of Legal Positivism: Law without Trimmings* (Oxford: Oxford University Press, 1999).
Marmor, A., 'Exclusive Legal Positivism', in Jules Coleman and Scott Shapiro (eds), *The Oxford Handbook of Jurisprudence and Philosophy of Law* (Oxford: Oxford University Press, 2002).
Morison, W. L., *John Austin* (London: Edward Arnold, 1982).
Postema, G. J., *Bentham and the Common Law Tradition* (Oxford: Clarendon Press, 1986).
Raz, J., *The Authority of Law* (Oxford: Oxford University Press, 1979).
—— *The Concept of Legal System: An Introduction to the Theory of Legal System* (2nd edn, Oxford: Clarendon Press, 1980).
—— *The Morality of Freedom* (Oxford: Oxford University Press, 1986).

——*Ethics in the Public Domain* (Oxford: Oxford University Press, 1994).
——*Practical Reason and Norms* (Oxford: Oxford University Press, 1999).
——*Engaging Reason: On the Theory of Value and Action* (Oxford: Oxford University Press, 2000).
——*Value, Respect, and Attachment* (Cambridge: Cambridge University Press, 2001).
Shapiro, S. J., *Legality* (Cambridge, MA: Belknap Press of Harvard University Press, 2011).
Tur, R. , and W. Twining (eds), *Essays on Kelsen* (Oxford: Clarendon Press, 1986).
Waldron, J. (ed.), *Nonsense upon Stilts: Bentham, Burke and Marx on the Rights of Man* (London: Methuen, 1987).
Waluchow, W. J., 'Authority and the Practical Difference Thesis: A Defence of Inclusive Legal Positivism' *Legal Theory* 6 (2000): 45, pp. 76–81.
——*Inclusive Legal Positivism* (1994).

Chapter 3: Dworkin: the moral integrity of law

Cohen, M. (ed.), *Ronald Dworkin and Contemporary Jurisprudence* (London: Duckworth, 1984).
Dworkin, R., *Taking Rights Seriously* (new impression with a reply to critics, London: Duckworth, 1978).
——*A Matter of Principle* (Cambridge, MA: Harvard University Press, 1985).
——*Law's Empire* (Cambridge, MA: Belknap Press, 1986).
——*Life's Dominion: An Argument about Abortion and Euthanasia* (London: HarperCollins, 1993).
——*Justice for Hedgehogs* (Cambridge, MA: Harvard University Press, 2011).
Guest, S., *Ronald Dworkin* (3rd edn, Palo Alto, CA: Stanford University Press, 2013).

Chapter 4: Rights and justice

Rights

Dworkin, R., *Taking Rights Seriously*, new impression with a reply to critics (London: Duckworth, 1978).

Dworkin, R., *A Matter of Principle* (Cambridge, MA: Harvard University Press, 1985).
Griffin, J., *On Human Rights* (Oxford: Oxford University Press, 2008).
Hohfeld, W. N., *Fundamental Legal Conceptions as Applied in Judicial Reasoning*, ed. W. W. Cook (Yale: Yale University Press, 1964; also in (1913) 23 *Yale Law Journal* 28).
Nussbaum, M., *Frontiers of Justice: Disability, Nationality, Species Membership* (Cambridge, MA: Belknap Press, 2006).
Simmonds, N. E., *Central Issues in Jurisprudence: Law, Justice, Law and Rights* (3rd edn, London: Sweet & Maxwell, 2008).
Waldron, J. (ed.), *Theories of Rights* (Oxford: Oxford University Press, 1984).
White, A. R., *Rights* (Oxford: Clarendon Press, 1984).

Justice

Daniels, N. (ed.), *Reading Rawls: Critical Studies on Rawls'* A Theory of Justice (Oxford: Basil Blackwell, 1975).
Hart, H. L. A., 'Between Utility and Rights', in H. L. A. Hart, *Essays in Jurisprudence and Philosophy* (Oxford: Clarendon Press, 1982).
Morawetz, T. (ed.), *Justice* (Aldershot: Dartmouth, 1991).
Nozick, R. T., *Anarchy, State, and Utopia* (Oxford: Basil Blackwell, 1974).
Polinsky, A. M., *An Introduction to Law and Economics* (London: Little, Brown & Co., 1983).
Posner, R. A., *The Economic Analysis of Law* (2nd edn, London: Little, Brown & Co., 1977).
—— *The Economics of Justice* (Cambridge, MA: Harvard University Press, 1981).
Rawls, J., *A Theory of Justice* (Oxford: Oxford University Press, 1973).
—— *Political Liberalism* (New York: Columbia University Press, 1993).
Raz, J., *The Authority of Law: Essays on Law and Morality* (Oxford: Clarendon Press, 1979).

Chapter 5: Law and society

Cain, M., and A. Hunt, *Marx and Engels on Law* (London: Academic Press, 1979).
Campbell, T., *The Left and Rights: A Conceptual Analysis of the Idea of Socialist Rights* (London: Routledge & Kegan Paul, 1983).
Collins, H., *Marxism and Law* (Oxford: Clarendon Press, 1982).

Cotterrell, R., *The Sociology of Law: An Introduction* (London: Butterworths, 1984).

—— *Law's Community: Legal Theory in Sociological Perspective* (Oxford: Clarendon Press, 1995).

Durkheim, É., *The Division of Labour in Society*, tr. George Simpson (London: Collier-Macmillan, 1964).

Hunt, A., *The Sociological Movement in Law* (London: Macmillan, 1978).

Kronman, A. R., *Max Weber* (London: Edward Arnold, 1983).

Lukes, S., and A. Scull (eds), *Durkheim and the Law* (London: Martin Robertson, 1983).

Marx, K., *Capital*, trans. B. Fowkes and D. Fembach (Harmondsworth: Penguin Books and Random House, 1976).

Weber, M., *The Religion of China: Confucianism and Taoism*, trans. and ed. H. H. Gerth (New York: Free Press, 1951).

—— *Max Weber on Law in Economy and Society*, ed. M. Rheinstein, trans. E. Shils and M. Rheinstein (Cambridge, MA: Harvard University Press, 1954).

—— *Economy and Society: An Outline of Interpretive Sociology*, ed. G. R. Roth and C. S Wittich (London: Bedminister Press, 1968).

Chapter 6: Critical legal theory

Realism

Duxbury, N., *Patterns of American Jurisprudence* (Oxford: Clarendon Press, 1995).

Fisher, W. W., M. J. Horwitz, and T. A. Reed (eds), *American Legal Realism* (Oxford: Oxford University Press, 1993).

Leiter, B., *Naturalizing Jurisprudence: Essays on American Realism and Naturalism in Legal Philosophy* (Oxford: Oxford University Press, 2007).

Llewellyn, K. N., 'Some Realism about Realism', *Harvard Law Review* 44 (1931): 1222.

Olivecrona, K., *Law as Fact* (2nd edn, London: Stevens & Sons, 1971).

Ross, A., *On Law and Justice*, trans. Margaret Dutton (London: Stevens & Sons, 1958).

Rumble, W. E., *American Legal Realism: Skepticism, Reform, and the Judicial Process* (New York: Cornell University Press, 1968).

Twining, W., *Karl Llewellyn and the Realist Movement* (London: Weidenfeld & Nicolson, 1973).

Critical legal studies

Boyle, J. D. A. (ed.), *Critical Legal Studies* (Aldershot: Dartmouth, 1992).

Kairys, D. (ed.), *The Politics of Law: A Progressive Critique* (London: Pantheon Books, 1982).

Kelman, M., *A Guide to Critical Legal Studies* (Cambridge, MA: Harvard University Press, 1987).

Norrie, A. (ed.), *Closure or Critique: New Directions in Legal Theory* (Edinburgh: Edinburgh University Press, 1993).

Unger, R., 'The Critical Legal Studies Movement', *Harvard Law Review* 96 (1983): 561.

—— *False Necessity: Anti-Necessitarian Social Theory in the Service of Radical Democracy* (Cambridge: Cambridge University Press, 1987).

Postmodern legal theory

Lacan, J., *The Four Fundamental Concepts of Psychoanalysis*, trans. A. Sheridan (Harmondsworth: Penguin, 1979).

Lyotard, J.-F. S., *The Postmodern Condition: A Report on Knowledge* (Manchester: Manchester University Press, 1984).

Patterson, D. (ed.), *Postmodernism and Law* (Aldershot: Dartmouth, 1994).

Rorty, R., *Philosophy and the Mirror of Nature* (Oxford: Basil Blackwell, 1990).

Feminist legal theory

Bartlett, K., 'Tradition, Change, and the Idea of Progress in Feminist Legal Thought' *Wisconsin Law Review* (1995): 303.

Gilligan, C., *In a Different Voice: Psychological Theory and Women's Development* (Cambridge, MA: Harvard University Press, 1982).

Kingdom, E. F., *What's Wrong with Rights? Problems for Feminist Politics of Law* (Edinburgh: Edinburgh University Press, 1991).

Lacey, N. (ed.), *Unspeakable Subjects: Feminist Essays in Legal and Social Theory* (London: Hart Publishing, 1998).

MacKinnon, C., *Feminism Unmodified: Discourses on Life and Law* (Cambridge, MA: Harvard University Press, 1987).

—— *Towards a Feminist Theory of the State* (Cambridge, MA: Harvard University Press, 1989).

Olsen, F. E., 'Feminism and Critical Legal Theory: An American Perspective', *International Journal of the Sociology of Law* 18 (1990): 199.

—— (ed.), *Feminist Legal Theory* (Aldershot: Dartmouth, 1994).
Rhode, D., *Justice and Gender: Sex Discrimination and the Law* (Cambridge, MA: Harvard University Press, 1989).
—— 'Feminist Critical Theories', *Stanford Law Review* 42 (1990): 617.
Scales, A., 'The Emergence of Feminist Jurisprudence: An Essay', *Yale Law Journal* 95 (1986): 1373.
Smart, P., *Feminist Jurisprudence* (Oxford: Clarendon Press, 1993).

Critical race theory

Delgado, R., and J. Stefanic, 'Critical Race Theory: An Annotated Bibliography' (1993) 79 *Virginia Law Review* 461.
—— (eds), *Critical White Studies: Looking Behind the Mirror* (Philadelphia, PA: Temple University Press, 1997).
Harris, A. P., 'Race and Essentialism in Feminist Legal Theory' *Stanford Law Review* 42 (1990): 581.

Index

A

B

C

D

E

I

J

K

L

M

S

T

U

V

W

LAW
A Very Short Introduction
Raymond Wacks

Law underlies our society - it protects our rights, imposes duties on each of us, and establishes a framework for the conduct of almost every social, political, and economic activity. The punishment of crime, compensation of the injured, and the enforcement of contracts are merely some of the tasks of a modern legal system. It also strives to achieve justice, promote freedom, and protect our security. This *Very Short Introduction* provides a clear, jargon-free account of modern legal systems, explaining how the law works both in the Western tradition and around the world.

www.oup.com/vsi